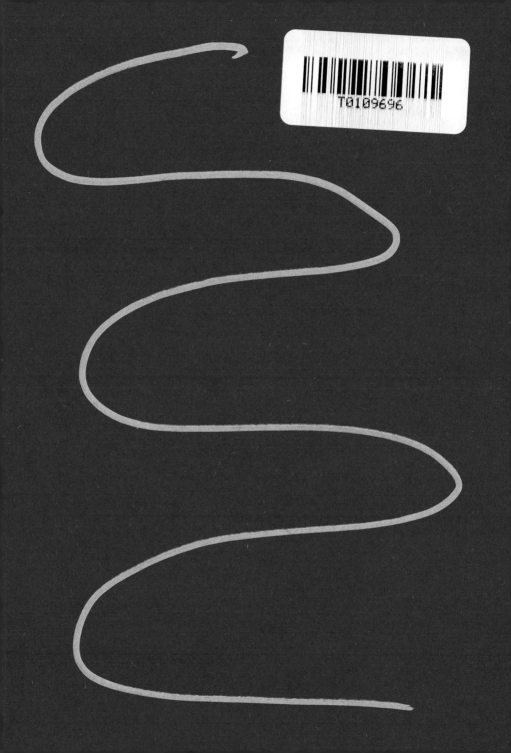

Adele Nozedar

Best selling Author of
The Hedgerow Handbook

FORAGING
with kids

52 Wild and Free Edibles to Enjoy with Your Children

Illustrations by
Lizzie Harper

NOURISH
EAT WELL, LIVE WELL

Foraging with Kids

Adele Nozedar

First published in the UK and USA in
2018 by Nourish, an imprint of Watkins
Media Limited, Unit 11, Shepperton
House, 89–93 Shepperton Road
London N1 3DF

enquiries@nourishbooks.com

Publisher: Jo Lal
Managing editor: Daniel Hurst
Editor: Emily Preece-Morrison
Cover designer: Georgina Hewitt
Designer: Karen Smith
Commissioned artwork: Lizzie Harper
Production: Uzma Taj

A CIP record for this book is available
from the British Library

ISBN: 978 1 78678 163 5

20 19 18 17 16 15 14 13 12 11

Typeset in Caecillia Std
Printed in the UK by TJ Books Ltd.

www.nourishbooks.com

CONTENTS

From Adele
Thanks to Dianne Davies, who was
my teacher at primary school; we are
still friends. Her wisdom, kindness,
imagination and wicked sense of humour
are utterly inspiring. I hope that everyone
knows at least one teacher like her.

From Lizzie
I'd like to dedicate this book to my
wonderful sister, Emily Harper, who is
supportive and wise, and knows more
about children and how to keep them
engaged, informed, and occupied than
anyone else I know.

Dear Foragers...

I'm hoping that many of the people reading this are children (yes – that means you!), or you may be a parent, guardian, uncle, aunt, grandparent, or possibly a teacher.

Whoever you are, no matter your age, or where you live, what kind of job you have or what kind of school you go to, whether you're tall or short, rich or poor – you all have one thing in common...

YOU ARE ALL FORAGERS!
Do I need to convince you? Okay, I'll explain exactly what a forager is, at least as far as this book is concerned. Ready?

Nearly everyone has – at one time in their life – picked a berry or a leaf from a plant growing in the wild and eaten it. That's foraging. To "forage" is to gather food in the wild (primarily plants, but also fungi) to eat, or use for medicine. This food can include leaves, flowers, fruit and berries, seeds, nuts, shoots and roots. Foraging doesn't concern itself with meat, although some foragers do regard certain shellfish and crustaceans as part of their harvest.

It's a vast subject. To simplify things for this book, I've decided to include only the plants that you are likely to see often, but maybe haven't paid much attention to before now. Lots of the plants will be ones that grow in your garden (even if they were never intended to be there). Some of the plants you'll know the names of, such as Nettles; others you won't, even if you see them every day. My editor Dan, for instance, was amazed to discover that the "stickyweed" that he used to chase his sister around with is also called Cleavers.

Foraging has become quite popular again and is something that many people do as a hobby, but it really wasn't THAT long ago that people had to gather wild plants in order to survive. These people would not have made long journeys to find rare and exotic plants; the most useful plants, and therefore the most valuable, would have been – and still are – the common ones that are plentiful and easy to find, right from home.

Let's try something: think of seven wild plants that you know, that you might guess to be edible ("edible" means you safely can eat them). They can be leafy plants; or ones with berries; they might be flowers; they could even be trees, some of which have nuts and blossoms. Write them down somewhere – just on a scrap of paper or whatever you have to hand.

I'm going to try to predict what might be on your list... so don't turn the page until you've finished selecting your seven plants.

Okay, let's see if I can guess some of the plants you've written down...

Nettles

Dandelions

Blackberries (or brambles)

Sloes

Wild Garlic

Rose Hips

Hazelnuts

Did I guess right? Even if none of these plants are the ones that you thought of, it doesn't matter – if you have written down the names of seven wild plants or their fruits, it shows that you know something!

And we know why that is...

It's because you're already a forager. You always have been and you always will be!

Still don't believe me? Let me explain further.

As a species, humans have foraged for at least 1.8 million years. I'm sure you'd agree that a habit this old isn't something that is easily lost. Human beings are resourceful, resilient and inventive; we are tool makers and problem solvers. When we go out into nature to look at plants, lots of the differences between ourselves and our ancestors fall away. In many instances, we are looking at exactly the same trees, shrubs and plants that they looked at. When we gather Wild Garlic from ancient woodlands, we are standing exactly where our ancestors stood hundreds – if not thousands – of years ago. When you touch the earth with your fingertips, or smell the freshness of wet mud after a rainy day, you are part of a long line of people, who have delighted in that same satisfying experience.

Nowadays, our lives are very full and we have lots of "stuff". So much, in fact, that getting rid of it (especially plastic) is becoming a massive problem. If my own grandparents could see how fast the world they knew has changed, they would be astonished. These changes, convenient though many are, have meant that our connection with the land, with where we are, has become fuzzier. But it's easy to regain that connection, and to realize what an incredible, awe-inspiring place this planet is. All we have to do is go outside.

You don't have to try to find all the plants in this book in one go – you won't be able to anyway, as they grow at different times and in different places. Pace yourself! If you feel like a break from foraging and fancy charging around a bit, maybe jumping in the odd puddle or climbing a tree, if you're good at that sort of thing, that's fine too. I want YOU to be the ones leading the way in your foraging adventures, with a little guidance from the grown-ups – not the other way round.

Now that we've established that, let me show you just how many wonderful wild plants can be found on your doorstep and the amazing things you can do with them.

Happy foraging! Adele

Safe Foraging

Here are a few safety points to consider when you go foraging:

• **KIDS** – do make sure that you are supervised at all times. Don't go foraging on your own, unless your parents or guardians have given you permission to do so.

• **Always ask a grown-up** before testing wild foods that you're not completely sure about.

• **When foraging,** it is likely that you will be trying food that you have never eaten before. Therefore, and especially if you are prone to allergies, it makes sense to try just a little of something first, as you would with any food.

• **ADULTS** – After trying a few wild foods, kids may be tempted to test other plants too (this is perfectly natural and small children, especially, will want to do this). If you are taking a younger person on a forage, be aware and keep a close eye on them.

REMEMBER – NOT ALL PLANTS ARE SAFE TO EAT!

The Names of Plants

Have you ever wondered how plants get their names? And did you know that most plants have more than one name? They have at least one common (or traditional) name and a botanical name.

Throughout the book, you will see that the heading for each plant includes the traditional or common name (which can have variations depending on where you live), and also the "official", botanical name, which remains the same, no matter what language is spoken, throughout the entire world. I have also included the names in several other languages, as I wanted to show that most of the plants you may think of as belonging to "your" country are actually quite at home around the world. I wish I could have included more!

1. Botanical names

Botanical names are universal. This means that whatever your native language, and no matter where you live, the official names for all plants (and animals, actually) are written in the same language – Latin.

The name for this way of describing plants and animals is called the "binomial system" ("bi" meaning "two"; "nomial" meaning "word"). This handy system was invented in the early part of the 18th century by an inspired Swedish botanist named Carl Linnaeus. Prior to Carl's system, scientists corresponding with one another couldn't be entirely sure that they were talking about the same plant. The new system also placed plants and animals into categories, or families, and helped make sense of the vast number of different species that inhabit this planet.

It is a testament to Linnaeus' smart thinking that the system is still in use today.

The first of the two names always starts with a capital letter and describes the "genus" (or general) name. The second word, which always starts with a lower-case letter, gives more detail. For example, the botanical name for the English Oak Tree is Quercus (which is the same for the entire Oak Tree family), followed by robur, which means "strength". Therefore, Quercus robur means "strong oak".

2. Common and traditional names

As well as the official common names, plants also have traditional or folk names. I've included some of these in the entries. It would be impossible to include all the names even for just one plant, as there are usually lots of regional variations or "pet" names for plants, some of which are very ancient indeed. Often the names are descriptive and tell you something about the plant. Sometimes, the names are a puzzle. Nevertheless, these names tell the story of the interaction between people and plants.

Let's take the Daisy (the small one that grows in grassy meadows and on lawns) as an example. The botanical name is Bellis perennis (Bellis means "pretty" and perennis means "everlasting").

The common name – Daisy – means "day's eye" (say it out loud), because the flower closes up when it gets dark and opens itself up in the sunshine.

And a traditional name for the Daisy is "bruisewort". The word "wort" is old, often used if a plant has been used either as a medicine or as food. And, yes, Daisies were once used to heal bruises – there's a recipe for a Daisy bruise ointment on p.191.

3. Your names... Finally, I've devised a third way of naming plants, which is entirely up to you!

The more you start to notice plants, the more fascinated by them you'll be. It's even possible that you may notice something that no-one else has noticed before.

Even if you're looking at a plant that you know really well, think about the first person that might have given it a name. Why would they have chosen that particular name? Maybe the name describes what the plant looks like, or how it behaves? Does it describe whether or not it is tasty? Or whether it might make cloth, or fodder for animals, or maybe a medicine of some kind? Don't forget to notice how the plant smells, or what the seeds look like. Does it like to grow in a particular place? Does it prefer light or shade? Like the Daisy, does it close up in the rain or in the dark? Does it appear all year round, or just in a particular season?

Although all these questions relate to the upper parts of plants, bear in mind that they have roots, too!

In this book, each plant entry gives you a space to make up your own name for the plant. You can write your name in the space (as long as the book belongs to you, and not to a friend or the library – if it does, jot down the name in your foraging logbook or notebook).

Once, I was taking a mixed group of children and adults out on a foraging walk. There was a very cheeky four-year-old who decided he wanted to lead the way and tell us all about the plants himself. The first one he came across was a Nettle, but he couldn't remember (or perhaps didn't know) that name. "They're Stingers!" he cried. I asked if he knew any other names. He thought for a moment. "Needle plant!" he shouted. He wasn't so far off the mark – it's thought that the word "Nettle" is indeed a derivation of the word "needle", referring, of course, to the stings.

In choosing your own names for plants, you're investing some of your own ideas and personality into another living creature; you're building up a relationship with the plant, and following in the footsteps of generations of people who did exactly the same thing.

Be as imaginative as you like. You could give your plant a secret name, that only you might understand. Or you could make sure that the name, although a new one, is one that describes the plant absolutely perfectly. Include words that describe the appearance and characteristics of the plant, as well as what it can do; then ask people if they can guess what it is!

Getting to Know Plants

There are lots of different ways you can use your senses to identify plants. Sight, touch, smell and – finally – taste, all come in to play.

SIGHT We can examine plants closely by looking. What colour is the plant? If green, what sort of shade? We can notice where they're growing and what kind of environment that is: are they in sun or shade; is the ground dry and dusty, or damp and wet; is it by the coast, or in a wooded area?

TOUCH The feel of a plant is also useful for identification. Are the stems and leaves smooth or hairy, for example? Does the plant have spines? Do the leaves have serrated edges?

SMELL Scent has an important part to play. If you crush the leaves of a plant, for example, what do they smell like? If they smell like nothing you've ever experienced, is that smell pleasant or nasty; medicinal or sweet?

TASTE Taste is always the last stage of identification. Don't try to nibble on something unless you are absolutely certain that your identification is accurate.

DRAWING PLANTS
The best way to learn to recognize plants is always to look at them very, very closely. Then, to have a go at drawing them. I asked Lizzie Harper, who illustrated this book and who looks closely at plants (and animals, and insects) all day long, to give us some tips.

Here's what she told me:
- A really brilliant way to learn about plants is to draw them. It doesn't make any difference whether you can scarcely hold a pencil, or if you're the second Leonardo da Vinci, it's the looking that counts.

- Draw what you actually see, rather than what you think is there (a good way to test this is to compare a drawing that you have done of a flower from your imagination with one that you have drawn when staring at an actual plant – you'll see an enormous difference).
- First, get paper and pencil and a rubber together. A magnifying glass can come in handy, too, and a plant identification book is helpful so you can name the plant once you've drawn it.
- Next, find a plant that interests you – be sure to consider the whole plant, down to the base of the stem. Set yourself up next to it and make sure you won't be distracted for half an hour.
- Start off by drawing a rough shape of the plant in light pencil on your paper, with a suggestion of where each leaf is and where the flowering parts are. Try to look at features such as the shape of the leaves and how they attach to the stem, how many petals or smaller flowers are involved in the flowering parts, and what the buds and fruit look like.
- Once you've got this light "map" down, you can start to add the detail. Look to see what the edges of the leaves do: are they smooth or have they got teeth? What direction do the leaf veins go in? What shape is each petal? Is the leaf smooth or hairy? Has the stem got spines on it, or is it smooth? Add these layers of information to your drawing.
- Have a think about why these traits might be there as you go along; is the flower coloured that way to attract insects? Why does the plant have to arm itself with thorns? What's the point of encasing a seed in a hard wooden nutshell? You'll have to stare and stare to sort out some of these details; this is where the learning happens – as you look so intently you'll find that you unconsciously learn how the plant is put together.
- Use the magnifying glass to sort out the details of things (like the middle of a flower or the tiny veins on a leaf). Feel free to pull the plant apart as you draw it; you're figuring out how it works, so you need to break it into its basic parts. Think of a mechanic at work on a motor, tinkering and taking it apart to see what's going on with each small bit of the whole engine. By understanding each element of a plant you learn how it works as a whole organism.

- I love this part of drawing, and find out incredible facts that blow me away. For example, finding out that each petal of the Wood Sorrel flower has the most delicate dark purple lines on it, which follow the veins that supply the petal with water and nutrients. Or realizing that the Common Daisy flower is actually two sorts of flowers; tiny yellow ones in the centre, and each white petal a perfect little white flower in its own right. (Go on, get that magnifying glass out, you'll see what I mean!) These things fill me with joy and wonder, and I'm sure your own drawing discoveries will do the same for you.
- Once you've drawn your plant, even if the resulting picture isn't a thing of beauty, you'll find you can instantly recognize that plant again. You'll have learned so much more about it than you ever could have done by just referring to a book. You'll know it inside and out, and this is because you'll have spent so long with it, staring at it, looking it, understanding it. All these things are required when you draw a plant, and that's why sketching plants is such a brilliant way to improve your plant identification skills.
- Even better, if you've drawn an edible plant, you can eat it when you're finished with your picture! This particularly appeals to the younger artists among us.
- **ONE LAST THING:** do NOT get hung up on whether or not you've made a good picture. The drawing itself is of secondary importance. The wonder and the glory of it all is that you've been lost in concentration and learning through looking, you've been drawing. And the best bit is that, the more you draw, the more you learn about plants and plant identification, and the better you get at drawing. What's not to like? Get those pencils sharpened and head out to find a plant right away!

Need a little help getting started? Why not colour in some of the illustrations in this book... Try to find the plant in nature and match the colours as closely as possible. This will help you think about how to approach your own drawings and also help with identifying the plant in the future.

Seasonal Calendar

The calendar overleaf and the key below will give you an idea of which parts of each plant are available at different times of the year, giving you an idea of what you can expect to find before you head out on your forage – just remember, just because something is in season does not guarantee that you will find it!

CALENDAR KEY:

ROOT & BULBS		STEM OR TRUNK	
LEAF		SEED	
BUDS & FLOWER		HARVEST*	
FRUIT			

*The harvest symbol is used to indicate the best time to pick fungi and coastal plants (where the whole plant is harvested at once). Be aware, though, that sometimes plants and fungi will stray outside these rules.

Plant Name	Early Spring	Late Spring	Early Summer	Late Summer	Early Autumn	Late Autumn	Early Winter	Late Winter
Bilberries (p.33)		flower	flower/leaf	fruit	fruit	shoot	shoot	shoot
Blackberries (p.36)		flower	flower·fruit	flower·fruit	flower·fruit	flower·fruit	shoot	shoot
Blackthorn (p.44)	flower	leaf	leaf	fruit	fruit	fruit	fruit	shoot
Bladderwrack (p.206)	seaweed	seaweed	seaweed	seaweed	seaweed	seaweed	seaweed	seaweed
Burdock (p.78)	root	leaf	leaf	leaf	leaf·root	leaf·root	leaf·root	leaf·root
Cauliflower Funghi (p.150)					fungi	fungi	fungi	
Chicken of the Woods (p.153)		fungi	fungi		fungi	fungi		
Chickweed (p.82)	shoot·leaf	shoot·leaf	shoot·leaf·flower	shoot·leaf·flower	shoot·leaf·flower	shoot·leaf	shoot·leaf	shoot·leaf
Cleavers (p.85)	shoot·leaf	shoot·leaf	shoot·leaf	shoot·leaf·flower	shoot·leaf·flower	shoot·leaf	shoot·leaf	shoot·leaf
Crab Apples (p.26)	shoot	flower	flower	fruit	fruit	fruit	fruit	fruit
Crow Garlic (p.169)		leaf·bulb	leaf·bulb					
Daisy (p.89)	leaf·flower	leaf·flower	leaf·flower	shoot·leaf·flower	shoot·leaf·flower	shoot·leaf·flower	leaf	leaf
Damsons (p.49)	shoot	flower	shoot·leaf·flower	leaf·fruit	leaf·fruit	leaf	shoot	shoot
Dandelion (p.92)	leaf	leaf·flower	leaf·flower	leaf·flower	leaf·flower	leaf	leaf	leaf
Douglas Fir (p.193)	shoot	shoot	shoot	shoot	shoot	shoot	shoot	shoot
Dulse (p.209)	seaweed	seaweed	seaweed	seaweed	seaweed	seaweed	seaweed	seaweed
Elder (p.54)	shoot	shoot·flower	leaf·flower	fruit	fruit	shoot·leaf	shoot	shoot
Fat Hen (p.99)	shoot·leaf	shoot·leaf	shoot·leaf	shoot·leaf·flower	shoot·leaf·flower	shoot	shoot	shoot
Giant Puffball (p.156)	fungi							fungi
Greater Plantain (p.102)	leaf	leaf	shoot·leaf	shoot·leaf·flower	shoot·leaf·flower	shoot·leaf·flower	shoot·leaf·flower	shoot·leaf·flower
Ground Elder (p.107)	leaf	leaf	leaf	shoot·leaf·flower	shoot·leaf·flower	shoot·leaf	shoot·leaf	
Ground Ivy (p.110)	leaf	leaf	leaf·flower	leaf·flower	leaf	leaf	leaf	leaf
Hairy Bittercress (p.171)	leaf	leaf·flower	leaf·flower	leaf·flower	leaf·flower	leaf·flower	leaf	leaf
Hawthorn (p.61)	shoot·leaf	leaf·flower	leaf·flower	leaf·flower	leaf·fruit	leaf·fruit	leaf	leaf
Heather (p.113)	shoot	shoot·leaf	shoot·leaf·flower	flower	flower	flower	shoot·flower	shoot
Horse Chestnut (p.189)	shoot	leaf	leaf·flower	leaf·flower	leaf·fruit	leaf·fruit	leaf	shoot

SEASONAL CALENDAR

Plant Name	Early Spring	Late Spring	Early Summer	Late Summer	Early Autumn	Late Autumn	Early Winter	Late Winter
Horseradish (p.117)	Stem	Leaf	Leaf	Leaf	Leaf	Leaf	Leaf	
Jack-by-the-Hedge (p.173)	Stem	Leaf	Leaf	Leaf, Buds&Flower	Leaf, Buds&Flower	Stem, Leaf	Stem, Leaf	Stem, Leaf
Laver (p.211)	Harvest	Harvest	Harvest	Harvest	Harvest	Harvest	Harvest	Harvest
Linden (p.199)	Stem	Leaf	Leaf	Leaf, Buds&Flower	Leaf	Leaf	Stem, Leaf	Stem
Mint (Corn) (p.124)	Stem	Stem	Leaf, Buds&Flower	Leaf, Buds&Flower	Leaf, Buds&Flower	Leaf	Stem	Stem
Mint (Water) (p.126)	Stem	Stem	Leaf, Buds&Flower	Leaf, Buds&Flower	Leaf, Buds&Flower	Leaf	Stem	Stem
Morel (p.159)		Harvest			Harvest	Harvest		
Nettles (p.130)	Stem	Stem, Leaf	Leaf	Leaf, Buds&Flower	Leaf, Buds&Flower, Seeds	Leaf, Seeds	Stem	Stem
Pineapple Weed (p.136)	Leaf, Buds&Flower	Leaf, Buds&Flower	Leaf, Buds&Flower	Leaf, Buds&Flower	Leaf, Buds&Flower	Leaf, Buds&Flower	Leaf	Leaf
Ramsons (p.180)	Stem	Leaf, Buds&Flower	Leaf, Seeds					Stem
Rock Samphire (p.214)	Leaf	Leaf	Leaf, Buds&Flower	Leaf, Buds&Flower	Leaf, Buds&Flower	Leaf	Leaf	Leaf
Rose (p.68)	Stem, Fruit	Stem, Leaf	Leaf, Buds&Flower	Leaf, Buds&Flower, Fruit	Leaf, Buds&Flower, Fruit	Leaf, Buds&Flower, Fruit	Leaf, Fruit	Stem, Fruit
Rosebay Willowherb (p.139)	Stem	Stem, Leaf	Leaf, Buds&Flower	Leaf, Buds&Flower, Seeds	Leaf, Buds&Flower, Seeds	Seeds	Stem, Seeds	Stem
Rowan (p.65)	Stem	Stem, Leaf	Leaf, Buds&Flower	Leaf, Buds&Flower	Leaf, Fruit	Leaf, Fruit	Leaf	Stem
Three-cornered Leek (p.177)	Leaf, Buds&Flower	Buds&Flower						Leaf
Scarlet Elf Cup (p.161)	Harvest							Harvest
Sea Beet (p.217)	Harvest	Harvest	Harvest	Harvest	Harvest	Harvest	Harvest	Harvest
Shaggy Ink Cap (p.164)	Harvest	Harvest		Harvest	Harvest	Harvest		
Sorrel (p.141)	Leaf	Leaf	Leaf	Leaf	Leaf	Leaf	Leaf	Leaf
Sweet Chestnut (p.196)	Stem, Leaf	Leaf, Buds&Flower	Leaf, Buds&Flower	Leaf, Buds&Flower	Leaf, Fruit	Leaf, Fruit	Leaf	Stem
Wild Cherries (p.30)	Stem	Buds&Flower	Buds&Flower	Fruit	Fruit	Stem, Leaf	Stem	Stem
Wild Marjoram (p.121)	Stem	Leaf	Leaf, Buds&Flower	Leaf, Buds&Flower	Leaf, Buds&Flower	Leaf, Buds&Flower	Stem, Buds&Flower	Stem, Buds&Flower
Wild Plums (p.47)	Stem	Leaf	Leaf, Buds&Flower	Leaf, Fruit	Leaf, Fruit	Leaf	Leaf	Stem
Wild Raspberries (p.41)	Stem	Stem, Leaf	Stem, Leaf, Buds&Flower	Leaf, Buds&Flower, Fruit	Leaf, Fruit	Leaf, Fruit	Stem	Stem
Wintercress (p.183)	Leaf	Buds&Flower	Buds&Flower	Buds&Flower				Leaf
Wood Sorrel (p.144)	Leaf	Leaf, Buds&Flower	Leaf	Leaf	Leaf	Leaf	Leaf, Buds&Flower	

KEY: ROOT & BULBS · LEAF · BUDS & FLOWER · FRUIT · SEEDS · HARVEST · STEM OR TRUNK

How to go Foraging

There's nothing complicated about going foraging! One thing is certain, though – you will need to go outside. If you have a garden, or a park close to your home, that's as good a place to start as any.

Check the weather forecast. You will need to wear footwear that is appropriate for the weather conditions and also for where you're planning to go. It's always a good idea to take a hat and maybe waterproofs, depending on the time of year or the forecast.

You can go foraging at any time of day, as long as it's light enough to see! You can also go foraging at any time of year – although, as you might expect, there are more plants around in the spring, summer and autumn (fall) months than in the winter. Have a look at the chart on p.16–17, which gives a guide to what is available and when.

All you need to do next is look around and see what you can find. Be aware that every single plant could be a contender. Sometimes, people look right past something tasty, often because they are so accustomed to seeing it every day that they actually don't notice it at all. Good examples of this are Cleavers (p.85), Nettles (p.130) and Dandelions (p.92). Don't take anything for granted.

Of course, not every single plant you see will be one that is included in this book, but many of the common ones are. Have a look through the book to see if there's a plant that you already recognize, then read all about it. The more you look and the more you read, the more you will learn.

What you will need
• **If you're very safety conscious,** you might like to pop a small pack of antibacterial or antiseptic wipes into your pocket (I have carried the same pack around with me for seven years now and still haven't needed to open it, although maybe one day I will). The same goes for plasters (band-aids), just in case you have a run-in with a thorn or two.
• **A camera** (maybe on a phone) is useful for taking pictures of plants or fungi, especially ones that you might not recognize yet. If you put

a coin next to the plant, including it in the picture, this will give you an idea of the scale for future reference.

- **A magnifying eyeglass** (sometimes called a loupe) is not essential, but certainly fun. They're cheap to buy online (get one with a 10 x magnification, 18mm/¾in lens). To use, put the lens as close to your eye as possible so that you can examine the tiniest aspects of your specimen. Minuscule hairs and leaf-patterns will be revealed clearly. Using a magnifying glass like this will open up a whole new world!
- **You will also need** to take something in which to carry your harvest. Plastic bags are not great because they cause plants to "sweat". A canvas or hessian bag, or a basket that you can sling across your chest, are all perfect (see also Further Resources on p.220).
- **You'll also need to take this book!** The more you forage, the more you will learn, and then you'll find that you'll want more books. I warn you that you may well start to spend quite a lot of money on books. There are some good online resources too, but I always prefer books (you can tell how much I like them by the number of times I've said "books" in this paragraph). Check out my reading list in Further Resources on p.220. Finally, find room in your pocket for a notebook and pencil. Use them to make a note of what you have found, including the date and time, and the habitat of the plant. Are the leaves unfurled? Is there a flower? How many petals? What colour is the stem? What colour are the leaves? Note as many details as you can in your foraging logbook. You can also use it to make drawings of your finds.

Where to go foraging

Here's a secret: you don't need to head off into remote rural areas or the wilderness to find plants. Although these places are generally teeming with plants and other wildlife, I have found that the best foraging to be had is generally in towns and cities.

Are you surprised? If you think about it, it makes sense. People use plants all the time. We plant them with the intention of cooking and eating them. We also plant them to make our gardens look nice, often without realizing that many "ornamental" plants are also edible. We turn plants into fabric or rope. We use them as dyes, to colour fabric. We use them as medicine. For thousands of years we have carried plants from one part of the planet to another; sometimes deliberately (such as the potato, which first came from South America) and sometimes by accident (lots of seeds are carried on the soles of our shoes, or in our trouser turn-ups, or even in our poo). So, it follows that in a place with lots of different people from lots of different places, there will also be lots of different kinds of plants, too. Cities, which are full of different nationalities, are GREAT places for foraging!

Having said that, some plants have preferred habitats. If you want to find coastal plants, you will need to go to the coast; if you want to find plants such as Heather or Bilberries, then you will need to head for the hills. Otherwise, I would advise that instead of going to look for something very specific, you might do better to start the other way around, by having a look around your immediate neighbourhood to see what is there. Sometimes, it can be a mistake to search for one specific thing, because we can miss several others in our single-mindedness.

Mindful foraging (or "foraging etiquette")

"Etiquette" is a French word, and means "polite behaviour". When we go foraging, it's important to remember that it's not just us humans that need plants to survive. Plants are vital to the entire animal kingdom. I have a feeling that you will be very aware of this anyway, so please forgive me if I'm telling you things that you already know. Here are a couple of polite foraging rules:

1 Only gather what you need, or can use. Tempting though it might be to pick a huge bagful of blackberries, if you're not going to use them it's wasteful. It also means that the wild creatures that rely on your harvest for their food will have missed out. When gathering leaves, take just a few from each plant, so that the plant can grow back.

2 Never be tempted to strip an entire tree, shrub, or indeed any plant, of all its flowers or fruits. Take a little from each plant, and no more than you need or can use. My own rule about Elderberries, for example, is to take only what I can comfortably reach; I don't use sticks or ladders to take anything higher up, as birds need them, and it feels wrong to do anything else. No-one is going to arrest you for picking berries from the top of the tree, so you have to rely on your own little voice inside to do what feels right, remembering what you already know about being a small part of a very much larger whole.

FRUIT,
BERRIES
& FLOWERS

About Fruit, Berries & Flowers

I looked at lots of different ways of putting the plants in this book into categories. At first, I thought it would be a great idea to make four sections, based around the seasons: spring, summer, autumn (fall) and winter. But I quickly realized that this could be troublesome – sometimes, different parts of a plant would belong in different seasons, which could be confusing. For example, consider one of my favourite plants, Elder; the flowers appear in one season (spring), but the berries appear in a different season (autumn/fall). Or how about the Dandelion? The leaves and flowers are harvested in the spring, but the roots are at their best later in the year. Then my editor Dan, who has had lots of great ideas about this book, pointed out that all the plants that have flowers or berries or other kinds of fruits would sit very nicely next to each other in their own chapter.

So here we are! Of course, the plants in this section might also fit elsewhere; Elder, for example, could also belong in the Trees chapter.

As you gain confidence in both foraging and cooking, I think it's likely that you may decide that plants with fruits, flowers and berries become your favourite ones to collect. Leaves are lovely, and tasty, and very good for you; berries, however, are a very versatile ingredient. You can bake them in pies, or make cordials from them, which in turn can be made into lollipops. Blackberries can be easily made into jam, Plums into a savoury sauce, Raspberries

All too often I have decided that I'll pick a certain fruit "next week", only to find that the birds have eaten them all, or that someone else got there before me!

into a sorbet (in fact, all these fruits/berries are interchangeable in the recipes). You have to bear in mind, though, that whilst the season for fruits is generous, it's still a good idea to gather them while you can. All too often I have decided that I'll pick a certain fruit "next week", only to find that the birds have eaten them all, or that someone else got there before me!

I'd also like to give you an important reminder. When harvesting flowers, do remember that many of these blossoms will become fruits. So never, never, *never* strip a tree of all its blooms. Something else I'd like to mention is to do with good foraging manners: birds, bees and other insects and animals rely on wild ingredients, so never take more than you need or can use.

Crab Apples
Malus sylvestris

Habitat: Hedgerows, fields, verges, open country, gardens

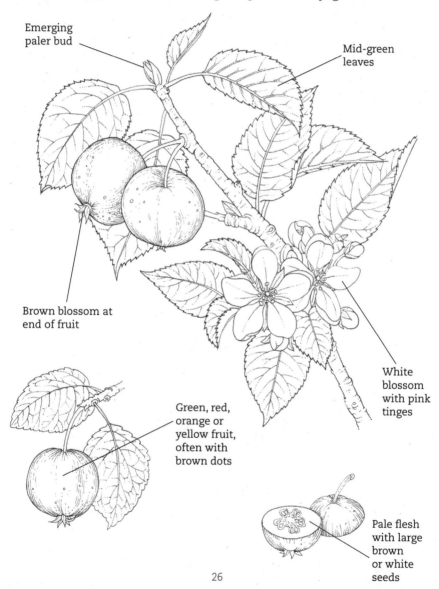

Emerging paler bud

Mid-green leaves

Brown blossom at end of fruit

White blossom with pink tinges

Green, red, orange or yellow fruit, often with brown dots

Pale flesh with large brown or white seeds

Apples are amazing. I love all kinds of apples, including the tiny little wild ones that we're talking about here. These little fruits are the ancestors of the "tame" apples that you usually buy in shops (unless, of course, you're lucky enough to have an apple tree in your neighbourhood or even in your garden). Lots of insects and other creatures rely on the Crab Apple tree (including the Eyed Hawk-moth, which eats the leaves). Butterflies, bees and hoverflies graze on the blossoms' nectar, and the apples themselves are eagerly munched by both birds (particularly thrushes and crows) and small mammals (foxes, voles and badgers).

The "crab" part of the name might well relate to the little seaside creatures that walk sideways. The origins of the name are not certain, but here are some of the most likely theories:

There's a Swedish word, skrabba, which means "unripe fruit". Crab Apples generally taste quite sharp and sour.

To be "crabby" or "sour" also means to be bad tempered (crabs certainly look bad-tempered to us humans, and have been known

> ### Names around the world
> **French** Pommiers sauvages
> **German** Holzapfel
> **Spanish** Manzanas sylvestres
> **Welsh** Afal bach surion
> **Polish** Jabłoń dzika, płonka
> **Swedish** Vildapel
> **Your name for this plant:**
>
> ....

to lash out with their claws). It follows that the sour-tasting apple might also have been called a "crabby" apple.

So, take your pick of these explanations, or have think and come up with your own story...! It could be just as valid as any other.

While it is true that people expect Crab Apples to be sour, this isn't always the case. The only way you can find out is to try them.

If you're really keen on discovering a sweet-tasting Crab Apple tree then you will have to get used to the toe-curling bitterness of nine out of ten trees at least. Sometimes, Crab Apples stay on the tree for the entire winter, hanging on through the harshest months of the year.

Try one of these older apples and you will find that they have a much mellower flavour than the younger ones – the cold weather encourages the sugars in the fruit to develop, hence the sweeter flavour.

Sour Crab Apples do have their uses though – they're full of pectin, the substance that helps jams and pickles to set. Rather than buy special pectin-enriched sugar for jam making, gather a quantity of Crab Apples instead. Chop them in half, remove the pips, add a little water and stew until tender. Let cool, then freeze the pulp in ziplock bags for using in preserves.

How can I recognize Crab Apples and where can I find them?

Crab Apple trees generally have quite an unruly, scruffy shape and, at full height, can reach up to 10m (32ft). They can live to be approximately 100 years old, so often become a feature of the landscape for several generations. Their leaves are a broad oval shape with serrations along the edges, about 10cm (4in) long.

In spring, a mass of white or pink blossoms, each with five white petals, can give away the whereabouts of the tree in a hedgerow, field or garden. In autumn (fall), the miniature apples are the tell-tale feature, although we need to be aware that not all Crab Apple fruits are the same! Some are small, the size of a marble, and some are a little larger, but they never grow as large as a "normal", cultivated apple. The colour varies, too; Crab Apples come in shades of red, yellow and green, or all three. Whatever the colour or size, the fresh apples are very hard.

Crab Apple trees can be found in hedgerows and fields and are sometimes planted in municipal places, such as shopping centres and car parks, or along verges next to roads in residential areas. There are also cultivated varieties which you might see at garden centres, developed specially to suit peoples' gardens.

Crab Apple Relish

A delicious homemade apple chutney that tastes great with cheese and crackers. You can use a mix of Crab Apples and baking apples, or even pears, if you like.

Makes 6 x 454-g (1-lb) jars

2kg (4½lb) crab apples (or a mixture of crab apples, baking apples or pears – see note in introduction)

400g (14oz/2 cups) soft brown sugar

2 large onions or 8 shallots, peeled and chopped into wedges

70g (2½oz/½ cup) raisins

10 cloves (count them)

10 green cardamom pods (count these too!)

10-cm (4-in) piece of fresh ginger, peeled and chopped

4 garlic cloves, peeled and chopped finely

500ml (17fl oz/2 cups) good-quality cider vinegar (this gives a smooth flavour)

2 tsp chilli flakes

2 tsp salt

❶ Chop the crab apples in half and remove the pips. If using, baking apples or pears should be peeled, pips removed and chopped into large chunks.

❷ Put all the ingredients into a large saucepan with a lid, stir to combine, and set over a low heat. Heat, stirring, until the mixture begins to bubble, then cover, turn the heat up a little and bring to the boil. Stir again, reduce the heat to low and cook, covered, for about 45 minutes.

❸ Remove the lid and cook for up to 45 minutes more, stirring occasionally and making sure that nothing "catches" on the bottom of the pan. The mixture will thicken and reduce in volume. Set aside to cool a little.

❹ Meanwhile, warm the sterilized jam (preserving) jars (see p.222 for sterilizing instructions) in a low oven for 5 minutes. Ladle the cooled relish into a jug, then pour it into the jars, not quite up to the top. Don't pour warm relish into a cold jar. Leave them to cool, then screw the lids on firmly.

❺ If kept unopened in the fridge, the relish should last for 6 months. Once opened, it should last for 1 month.

Wild Cherries
Prunus avium

Habitat: Open areas, hedgerows, roadsides, parks, gardens

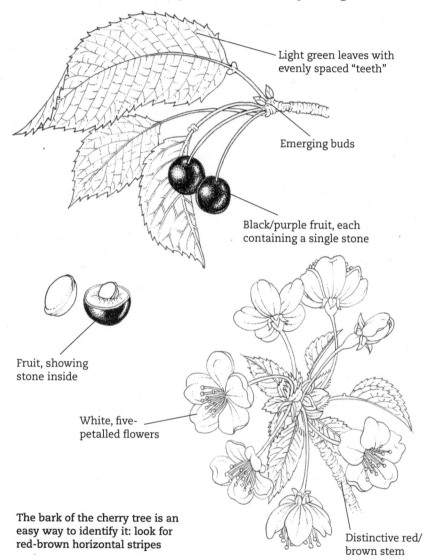

Light green leaves with evenly spaced "teeth"

Emerging buds

Black/purple fruit, each containing a single stone

Fruit, showing stone inside

White, five-petalled flowers

The bark of the cherry tree is an easy way to identify it: look for red-brown horizontal stripes

Distinctive red/brown stem

The name of this tree, Prunus avium, means "bird cherry" in Latin, referring to the birds who help to propagate (which means "spread") the tree – the birds eat the cherries, containing the seeds, and then spread them far and wide in their droppings. Blackbirds, thrushes and lots of different caterpillars rely on this tree, and its fruits, for food.

Cherry wood is popular with furniture makers, since it is very hard and strong, and polishes to the colour of dark honey.

How can I recognize Wild Cherries and where can I find them?

Preferring a sunny position and good soil, the Wild Cherry tree grows to 30m (98ft) high and can live for 60 years. The bark is a distinctive dark red-brown colour, quite glossy, with horizontal bands along the trunk. Its leaves are green, oval and pointed, about 6–15cm (2½–6in) long, and turn a bright orange/red before falling in the autumn (fall). When the tree is in full flower, it is a beautiful sight – masses of the white, fluffy, five-petalled blossoms cover it, soon replaced by the smooth, deep red

> ## Names around the world
> **French** Cerisier des oiseaux
> **German** Vogel-kirschen
> **Spanish** Cerezas silvestres
> **Welsh** Ceirios
> **Polish** Wiśnia dzika, Czereśnia
> **Swedish** Körsbär
> **Your name for this plant:**
>
> ....

or black cherries, which are held on long stalks.

Each cherry contains a small, hard stone. It is easiest to spot Wild Cherry trees from a distance by the blossom, and then by the fruit. Always remember to look up when foraging, as well as looking on the ground – the cherries also fall from the tree! You'll find Wild Cherry trees in woodlands and hedgerows, where birds have dropped the stones and the trees have sprouted up.

You may see ornamental Cherry trees in gardens. Despite the word "ornamental", their fruit is still edible, although the flavour will vary – the cherries may be very sweet, or may be quite tart.

Wild Cherry Pie

I collected the Cherries for this pie from a stand of at least ten trees growing set back from a quiet roadside. Try the Cherries first to see how they taste.

Serves 6–8

FOR THE PASTRY:

350g (12⅓oz/2⅔ cups) plain (all-purpose) flour, plus extra for dusting

180g (6⅓oz/generous ¾ cup) butter, at room temperature

100g (3½oz/scant ¾ cup) icing (confectioners') sugar

pinch of salt

pinch of ground nutmeg (optional)

3 egg yolks

2 tbsp ice-cold water

FOR THE FILLING:

1kg (35oz) wild cherries, pitted

100–350g (3½–12⅓oz/½–1¾ cups) caster (superfine) sugar

1 tsp cornflour (cornstarch)

1 tsp orange or apple juice

1 tsp demerara (turbinado) sugar

❶ For the pastry, put all the ingredients except for the egg yolks and water into a food processor and whizz until it looks just like breadcrumbs. Add the egg yolks, pulse a few times to blend, then add the ice-cold water, drop by drop, until the mixture comes together. Turn the dough onto a floured work surface and give it a quick knead. Pop into a plastic bag and chill for 1 hour.

❷ Meanwhile, put the cherries into a mixing bowl, add the sugar a little at a time and taste; add more sugar if you need it. Add the cornflour (cornstarch) and juice and leave to stand.

❸ Preheat the oven to 160°C/325°F/Gas Mark 3. Lightly butter a 20-cm (8-in) pie dish. Remove the dough from the fridge and cut it in half. Dust the work surface with icing (confectioners') sugar and roll half of the dough into a circle large enough to line the pie dish. Line the dish with the pastry and heap the cherry filling on top. Roll out the remaining pastry to a 20-cm (8-in) circle, then lay it on the top of the cherries. Press down the edges to seal. Make a series of 5 or 6 small slits in the pastry, brush with water and sprinkle the demerara (turbinado) sugar over the top.

❹ Bake in the hot oven for about 30 minutes, turning once, until golden brown. Leave to cool and serve with cream or ice cream.

Bilberries
Vaccinium myrtillus

Habitat: Hilly, remote areas, acid soil

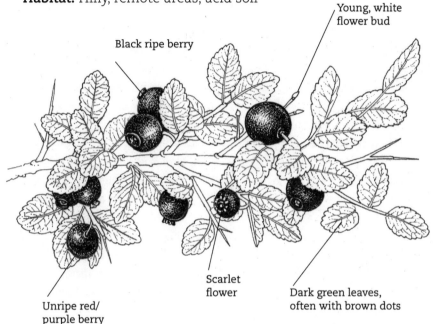

Black ripe berry

Young, white flower bud

Scarlet flower

Unripe red/ purple berry

Dark green leaves, often with brown dots

There are lots of different pet names for Bilberries. You might hear them referred to as Wimberries, Whinberries, Blaeberries, Whortleberries, Hurts, Huckleberries, or – and this is my favourite, since it's what we used to call them in Yorkshire where I come from – "Mucky Mouth". This is because, if you eat lots of them, they temporarily stain

Names around the world

French	Myrtilles
German	Heidelbeeren
Spanish	Arándanos
Welsh	Llus, Llusi duon bach
Polish	Czarna jagoda
Swedish	Blåbär

Your name for this plant:

....

your teeth and lips black. The Blueberries that you can buy in plastic boxes in supermarkets are the commercially-grown relatives of the wild Bilberry, and although they taste OK, they're not nearly half as tasty as the wild ones, which explode in your mouth in a mixture of tanginess, juiciness and sweetness.

As well as tasting amazing, Bilberries are rich in vitamin C. At one time, harvesting Bilberries during the summer months was a good way for people living in the countryside to earn some extra money, by selling the fruits to restaurants. It's not so very long ago that entire families would head up to the hills with their baskets, using a special tool called a Wimberry comb – a deep scoop-shaped tool, with a series of narrow prongs at the front, which drag along the plants to grab the fruits efficiently. The old kind were made of wood, and you can buy modern plastic versions. However, sometimes these combs can damage the plant by tearing the roots. Although it is cheaper and easier for restaurants to buy commercially-grown Blueberries, some foragers still pick the wild fruits to sell to the best restaurants since their monetary value as a local delicacy can be quite high.

How can I recognize Bilberries and where can I find them?

These dark, shiny little berries like to grow in really wild places, usually in hilly upland areas of acidic soil, in the same sort of conditions favoured by Heather. In fact, both Bilberries and Heather belong to the "Ericaceous" family of plants. Bilberries have woody, wiry stems, grow up to 50cm (20in) high, and have small oval leaves with a smooth, leathery texture. These leaves turn red in the autumn (fall) before they fall, leaving behind a tangle of skinny, woody stems. Before the fruit comes, the flowers appear; these are pinkish green and bell-shaped. The berries ripen at different times of the year, depending on what part of the world you live in, but usually in late summer. The berries are a deep purple/blue/black colour, up to 1cm (½in) wide (although they're usually smaller than this), and have a smooth flat disc shape on their tops.

Fraughan Pie

The old Irish name for the berries is "Fraughan", so the day for picking was called "Fraughan Sunday". Traditionally, the berries were made into a pie – a celebration of the harvest of a well-loved and delicious free fruit.

Serves 6–8

FOR THE PASTRY:

250g (9oz/2 cups) plain (all-purpose) flour, plus extra for dusting

1 tbsp icing (confectioners') sugar, plus extra if needed

150g (5½oz/⅔ cup) butter, chilled and cut into very small cubes

½ tsp lemon juice

100ml (3½fl oz/generous ⅓ cup) very cold water

1 egg white, beaten

FOR THE FILLING:

75g (2⅔oz/generous ⅓ cup) caster (superfine) sugar, plus 2 tbsp for sprinkling

1 level tbsp cornflour (cornstarch) or finely ground almonds

500g (18oz/4 cups) bilberries

❶ Sift the flour and icing (confectioners') sugar into a large bowl. Add the butter and rub into the mixture with the tips of your fingers. Mix the lemon juice into the water and add it, a little at a time, to the flour mixture. Bring the dough together, adding extra icing sugar if it feels too sticky. Then, put the dough into a plastic bag and chill for up to an hour.

❷ Meanwhile, mix together the sugar and cornflour (cornstarch) or almonds in a large bowl.

❸ Put a thin layer of the berries into a 22-cm (8½-in) pie dish and sprinkle a layer of the sugar mixture over the top. Repeat until the berries and sugar are used up.

❹ Preheat the oven to 220°C/425°F/Gas Mark 7. Flour a clean work surface and roll out the pastry to 5mm (¼in) thick.

❺ Rub a little water around the edge of the pie dish, then drape the pastry over the fruit, pressing down the edges to seal. Brush the egg white over the top, then sprinkle over the extra sugar and make 3 small cuts in the pastry.

❻ Bake for about 15 minutes, then reduce the heat to 180°C/350°F/Gas Mark 4 and bake for up to 30 minutes more, until an even golden colour all over.

❼ Let the pie cool for 15 minutes before serving with ice cream, Greek yogurt or crème fraîche.

Blackberries
Rubus fruticosus

Habitat: Anywhere and everywhere

At first the fruit is bright green, then red, then, finally, black

Green leaves in "sets" of three or five

The "berry" is in fact made from lots of tiny berries, each with its own seed. These are called "drupelets".

Ripe and unripe fruit often appear on the same bush, meaning brambles have a long season

Tough, thorny stems

Five-petalled flowers that are white with touches of pink

Blackberries are, for lots of us, the first wild plant that we learn to pick. Gathering them makes you part of a tradition that goes back for thousands of years. They're delicious, abundant and, above all, easy to recognize. There is nothing which can be mistaken for a Blackberry. At first small and green (and quite hard), the berries travel through a colour spectrum of pink, red, purple and finally black, as they ripen. Their season is a long one, and it's common to see both the blossoms and the fruit, all at different stages of ripeness, on the same arching briar.

Blackberries are loved by wildlife, too. Deer like to graze on the leaves, the berries are eaten by birds and foxes and the blossoms are favoured by a whole host of bees, butterflies and other insects.

An ancient folk belief says that you shouldn't eat Blackberries after October 11th, since mischievous spirits spoil them after that date by spitting on them. In truth, at that time of year the weather is getting colder and the berries themselves are usually past their best and sometimes starting to go mouldy.

If you've ever got caught up in these thorny branches whilst picking the fruits, or if you've helped remove them from places where they're not wanted in the garden, you'll know just how sharp and prickly they are. Centuries ago, they were used to mark boundaries (and keep people out) in exactly the way that we use barbed wire today. They're often found in churchyards, where, some people say, they were once deliberately planted to keep sheep out.

> ## Names around the world
>
> **French** Mûres sauvages
>
> **German** Brombeeren
>
> **Spanish** Moras
>
> **Welsh** Mwyaren or mwyar duon
>
> **Polish** Jeżyna krzewiasta
>
> **Swedish** Björnbär
>
> **Your name for this plant:**
>
> ....

How can I recognize Blackberries and where can I find them?

In their first year of growth, thorny Blackberry canes (sometimes called "brambles") can grow up to 9m (30ft) in length, arching through thickets, catching your clothes and hair, scratching your skin and sometimes even tearing little holes in your clothes. These long stems can be either green or red, bearing leaves that are made of three to five smaller leaflets. It is in the second year of growth that this plant becomes more interesting to foragers, since it is then that the pinkish-white five-petalled blossoms appear. These blossoms make way for the delicious black fruits that stain your hands, clothes, and anything else they come into contact with, deep purple. Although we refer to them as berries, the fruits of the Blackberry are, strictly speaking, a collection of little individual parts called "drupelets" that make up the whole fruit. Each of these tiny drupelets contains a small pip, which can get stuck in your teeth, especially if you make Blackberry jam.

Can you think of another fruit that has drupelets?[1]

Blackberries don't mind poor soils or growing conditions that other plants might not be able to cope with; this means that they will grow pretty much anywhere and everywhere. You'll see them in forests and woods, in soggy ditches, in dry and dusty wasteland, in hedgerows, and often lurking in untended corners of gardens. They scramble across cliffs at the coast and pop up in abandoned city areas.

So, what to do with all those Blackberries you've picked? There's a good chance you might have eaten quite a few by the time you get home! They freeze very well, but make sure there's room in the freezer before you go out and pick lots more. The following pages have some great recipes to try out.

This makes a delicious and filling snack to put in a lunch box.

Makes 12 pieces (or more, if you cut them smaller!)

250g (9oz/generous 2 cups) self-raising (self-rising) flour

250g (9oz/1¼ cups) soft brown (light muscovado) sugar

30g (1 oz/⅔ cup) porridge oats (rolled oats)

pinch of salt

200g (7oz/1¾ sticks) butter, cold, chopped into small pieces

80g (3 oz/1 cup) dessicated (dried shredded) coconut, preferably unsweetened

2 medium eggs, beaten

350g (12oz/generous 2½ cups) blackberries, fresh or frozen

Blackberry and Coconut Traybake

❶ Preheat the oven to 180°C/350°F/Gas Mark 4. Grease and line a 13 x 17 x 5cm (5 x 7 x 2in) baking pan with baking parchment.

❷ Put the flour, sugar and oats into a large bowl, along with a small pinch of salt. Then, using only the tips of your fingers, rub the butter into the mixture until it resembles breadcrumbs. Add the coconut to the bowl and stir thoroughly to combine. Fill a teacup or small mug with some of the mixture and set aside to sprinkle on top later.

❸ Gently stir the beaten eggs into the remaining mixture, then spoon it all into the lined baking pan, using the back of a spoon to make sure the surface is level. Spread the berries all over the top, then sprinkle over the reserved crumble mixture, making sure that all the fruit is covered.

❹ Bake in the hot oven for 1 hour 15 minutes, until golden, turning the pan after 40 minutes to make sure that it bakes evenly. Leave to cool in the pan, then cut into squares. They will keep for 1 week in an airtight container.

Easy Blackberry Jam

Sometimes, when foraging, I make jam – outside, on a camping stove. I pour it into jars and give them to people to take home. The particular method required to make this jam is not exactly conventional, so here's a more sensible recipe, which is easy for you to make at home!

Makes 8 x 340-g (12-oz) jars

1.8kg (4lb) ripe fresh blackberries
80ml (2½fl oz/5 tbsp) apple juice
freshly squeezed juice of 2 lemons
1.8kg (4lb) granulated sugar

❶ Before you do anything, put a saucer into the freezer (you'll find out why soon enough!).

❷ Rinse the berries in a sieve (fine-mesh strainer), drain well, and pick out any scraps of leaves.

❸ Put the fruit, apple juice and lemon juice into a heavy saucepan with a lid and set over a very low heat. Cook, covered, for about 1 hour, until the fruit is pulpy. Make sure it doesn't burn.

❹ Add the sugar and stir with a wooden spoon. Gradually bring the mixture to the boil; the liquid may spit, so be very careful. Let it boil for 5 minutes. Take the saucer out of the freezer. Carefully spoon a little blob of the jam onto it, wait for 30 seconds, then push it gently with the tip of your finger. If it wrinkles on top, the jam is ready. If it doesn't, keep boiling and test every minute or so.

❺ As soon as it's ready, turn off the heat and leave the jam to cool down for about 20 minutes.

❻ Meanwhile, warm the sterilized jam (preserving) jars (see p.222 for sterilizing instructions) by heating in a low oven for 5 minutes.

❼ Ladle the cooled jam into a jug, then pour it into the jars, not quite up to the top. Set aside, uncovered, until the jam is completely cold, then screw the lids on firmly. If kept unopened in the fridge, the jam should last for 6 months. Once opened, it should last for 1 month. If white "blobs" appear on top of the jam, just remove them with a spoon – the jam underneath will be fine.

Wild Raspberries
Rubus idaeus

Habitat: Forested areas, wooded high ground

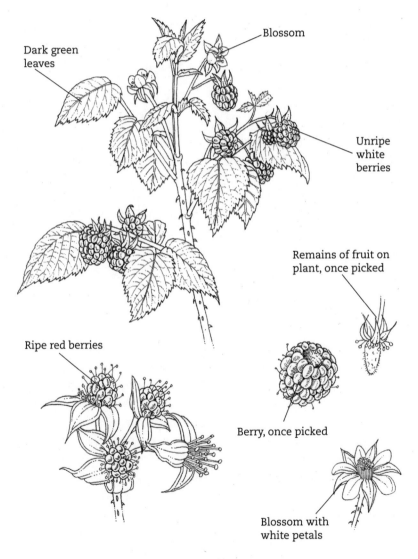

Blossom

Dark green
leaves

Unripe
white
berries

Remains of fruit on
plant, once picked

Ripe red berries

Berry, once picked

Blossom with
white petals

How can I recognize Wild Raspberries and where can I find them?

The fruits of a Wild Raspberry look very much like Blackberries, except more elongated and, of course, unlike Blackberries (which are black when ripe), Raspberries are bright red when ready to eat. The leaves are similar to those of Blackberries, too; carried on straight stems, they consist of three to five leaflets, with serrated edges. Whereas the Blackberry plant has a sprawling habit, Wild Raspberries grow in clumps of tall canes up to 2.5m (8ft) high.

Raspberry canes can be found at the edges of forests and in the clearings, too. They also appear along roadsides and tracks in places where forestry is planted, generally on higher ground. If you've seen Cultivated Raspberries, you'll know that the fruits can grow to 1.5cm (¾ in) in length, sometimes larger. Wild Raspberries are smaller, about half the size, and much sweeter.

In the winter, the canes look like thin, scruffy sticks; the leaves start to appear in the spring; then the white five-petalled blossoms; then the most exciting part,

Names around the world

French Framboisiers
German Himbeeren
Spanish Frambuesas
Welsh Mafon
Polish Maliny
Swedish Hallon

Your name for this plant:

....

the sparkling red fruits. These fruits appear in the summer and continue into the autumn (fall) if the weather is mild. The plants have creeping, perennial roots, sending up suckers that increase the number of the plants. The "ideaus" part of the name is Greek; it refers to Mount Ida, that was once famous for the crops of Wild Raspberries that grew there.

When you pick Wild Raspberries, as you pull gently at the fruit, the white "core" of the berry stays on the stem – you eat the red bobbly part that's left in your hand. Although there are plenty of recipes that you can make using Raspberries, they are so delicious that it's hard not to eat them straight from the cane!

Raspberry Shrub

A "shrub", whilst also being the name for a bushy plant, is also the name (of ancient origin) for a drink containing fruit, sugar, ice and... vinegar! Once upon a time, this name was much more exotic. It started out as "Shariba", an Arabic name, which is also the origin of the words "sherbet" and "sorbet", as well as "shrub".

Makes 1.5l (50fl oz/6¼ cups)

500g (18oz/3⅓ cups) raspberries
350g (12oz/1¾ cups) caster (superfine) sugar
1l (34fl oz/4¼ cups) good-quality apple cider vinegar
sparkling water, to serve
handful of fresh mint leaves, to garnish

❶ Put the raspberries into a large bowl (use glass, stainless steel or china, as certain types of metal spoil the taste of soft fruits). Mash with a wooden spoon for a few minutes, to break up the fruits. Add the sugar, stir to combine, then cover and leave overnight in a cool place (but not the refrigerator).

❷ Next day, pour the vinegar into the fruit/sugar mixture and stir again with a wooden spoon. Leave for 1 hour, then strain the mixture through a fine-mesh sieve (strainer) into a jug (pitcher), pushing as much of the fruit through as you can. There shouldn't be too much pulp.

❸ Serve diluted with sparkling water and with a sprig of fresh mint to garnish.

❹ If you keep it in the freezer, your delicious shrub will last indefinitely. Store it in plastic water bottles, leaving a little space at the top of the bottle so that the liquid has space to expand as it freezes. It will also keep for up to a year in the refrigerator.

If you need to, collect the fruit in batches, freezing them until you have enough for the recipe. Also, please don't be tempted to use malt vinegar – your shrub will taste horrible!

Blackthorn (Sloes)

Prunus spinosa

Habitat: Hedgerows, verges, wasteland

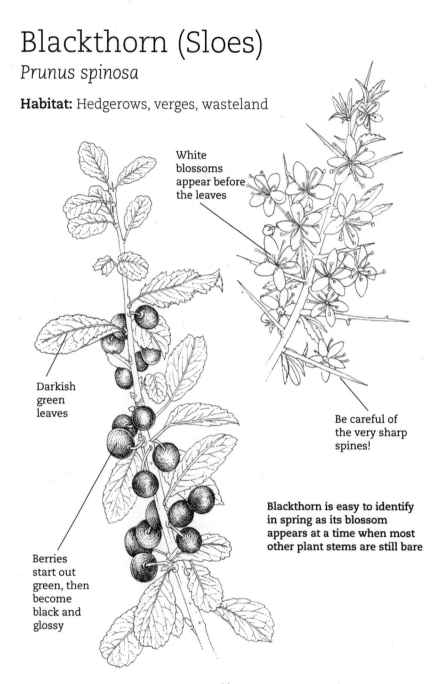

White blossoms appear before the leaves

Darkish green leaves

Be careful of the very sharp spines!

Blackthorn is easy to identify in spring as its blossom appears at a time when most other plant stems are still bare

Berries start out green, then become black and glossy

SLOES, WILD PLUMS AND DAMSONS

I've grouped these three plants together, since they're closely related and grow in similar conditions. Often, different varieties of these fruits cross-fertilize to make a new variety. Other members of this particular family include Greengages and Cherry Plums.

When we talk about foraging for Blackthorn, what we're really after are the fruits, which are called Sloes. But to find Sloes, we first need to be able to identify the tree that they grow on!

How can I recognize Blackthorn and where can I find it?

Blackthorn is a cross between a large bush and a small tree, growing to about 5m (16ft) tall, if left untrimmed (as it is a popular hedgerow plant, it is often cut back and shortened). Blackthorn has small oval leaves and is easy to recognize in the early spring, since its white flowers appear before the leaves. (Hawthorn (p.61), which can often be found growing next to Blackthorn, works the other way round; the leaves come before the flowers.)

Names around the world

French	Prunellier, Prunelles
German	Schlehen
Spanish	Endrinas
Welsh	Eirin perthi (hedge plums)
Polish	Śliwa tarnina
Swedish	Slånbär

Your name for this plant:

....

On a mild day in early spring, take a moment to inhale the fragrance of the Blackthorn flowers; they smell, and taste, faintly of almonds.

The tangled twigs of this shrub feature very hard, sharp spines, with a needle-thin end that can

45

penetrate the skin very easily. These spines are so sharp that at one time they were used to pin timber together, so do be very careful to watch out for them! If you do get one badly stuck in your skin, it's best to see a doctor, who will be able to check that there's no infection.

It's because of these tangled branches and sharp spines, as well as the fact that it grows quickly, that Blackthorn has been used for thousands of years to make hedges and safe enclosures for animals. The fruits of the Blackthorn are called Sloes. When ripe – in the late autumn (fall) and winter – they are very sour-tasting indeed, enough to make your tongue feel like it is shrivelling up, and therefore not particularly nice to eat on their own.

Traditionally, they are used to make a concoction called Sloe Gin (which I think tastes a bit like cough medicine), however, their sourness blends really well with their sweeter-tasting cousins (see recipe on p.53).

Wild Plums
Prunus domestica

Habitat: Hedgerows, verges, wasteland, domestic gardens

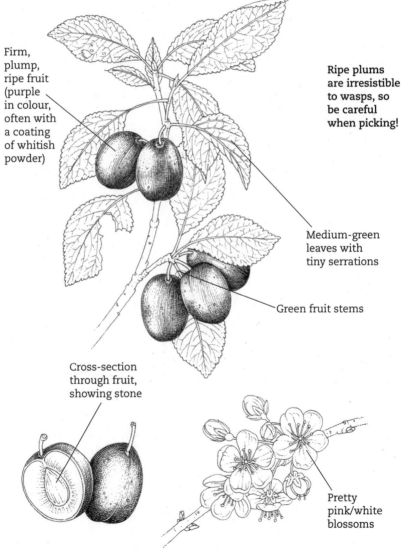

Firm, plump, ripe fruit (purple in colour, often with a coating of whitish powder)

Ripe plums are irresistible to wasps, so be careful when picking!

Medium-green leaves with tiny serrations

Green fruit stems

Cross-section through fruit, showing stone

Pretty pink/white blossoms

How can I recognize Wild Plums and where can I find them?

Left to its own devices, a Wild Plum tree is somewhat sprawling, stretching to a height of 12m (39ft) and with a spread not much smaller, at 10m (33ft). However, just like Blackthorn trees, Wild Plum trees are often pruned, especially since they're often found in hedgerows or at boundaries. The leaves of the tree are a simple oval shape with tiny serrations along the edges, coming to a point at the end. Blossom appears in the spring; it looks a lot like apple blossom, pink/white with five petals. The fruits themselves appear later in the year. Initially hard green balls, plums grow softer, plump and juicy, up to 7cm (3in) long, and turn a purple colour. There's often a whitish powder on their skins; this "bloom" is down to natural yeasts, and is nothing to worry about.

There are lots of different varieties of Plum, wild or not; some are purple, some are yellow, some are pink, and Greengages – yet another species – are green. They all have one thing

Names around the world

French Prunier Commun
German Pflaumen
Spanish Ciruelas
Welsh Eirin
Polish Śliwki
Swedish Plommon
Your name for this plant:

....

in common, though – slice the fruit in half and you'll find a hard stone inside.

Have you ever had prunes, maybe mixed with yogurt as a breakfast dish? They're dried plums! And in China, salted plums make for a popular snack.

Damsons
Prunus insititia

Habitat: Hedgerows, verges, wasteland, domestic gardens

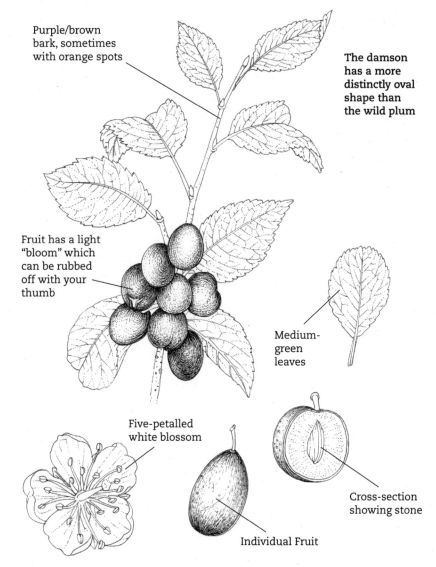

Purple/brown bark, sometimes with orange spots

The damson has a more distinctly oval shape than the wild plum

Fruit has a light "bloom" which can be rubbed off with your thumb

Medium-green leaves

Five-petalled white blossom

Individual Fruit

Cross-section showing stone

How can I recognize Damsons and where can I find them?

Yet another species of the Plum tree, the name of this fruit is derived from the word "Damascene", meaning "from Damascus", the capital of Syria. In appearance they're very much like the Wild Plum (p.47), although tend to be smaller, and the tree bears fruit at an older age than the Plum. Another difference is its flavour; when ripe, it has both a sweet and sharp flavour which makes for a lovely jam.

A true Damson has an oval shape, coming to a point at the opposite end from the stalk. The fruits come in different colours: blue-purple, yellow or green.

In Britain, Damsons were at one point planted as wind protection for apple orchards as well as planted in orchards in their own right.

After the war, farming methods changed dramatically and a lot of the trees were dug up so that farmers could fill the fields with other crops, including wheat.

Names around the world

French	Prunier de Damas
German	Damaszenerpflaumen
Spanish	Ciruelas damascena
Welsh	Eirinen Hir, Eirinen Ddamasg
Polish	Śliwa domowa lubaszka, Śliwka węgierka
Swedish	Krikon

Your name for this plant:

....

Damson orchards, grown specifically for making jam, were once a common sight before the Second World War.

Poached Plums/ Damsons

The following two recipes were given to me by Suzanne Davies, a chef. I first met her when we were asked to work together at the Llangynidr Show in South Wales. After that we became good friends!

If you're lucky enough to find a glut of Plums and Damsons, then this is a great way of using the fruits. You need to make the Poached Plums/Damsons before you can make the Spicy Plum/ Damson Sauce (p.52).

Makes 2 x 450g (1lb) jars

1kg (2¼lbs) fresh or frozen plums (or
    damsons), washed
500g (18oz/2½ cups) granulated sugar

❶ Place the plums or damsons in a large heavy saucepan, add the sugar and just enough water to come halfway up the fruit.

❷ Set over a medium heat and stir until the sugar is dissolved, then cover and simmer for 15–20 minutes, until the fruit is tender.

❸ Strain the poached fruit in a sieve (strainer) set over a measuring jug. Take 500ml (17fl oz/2 cups) of the syrup and set aside for use in the Spicy Plum/ Damson Sauce recipe (see p.52).

Let the fruit cool, then pick out and discard the stones. The remaining syrup can now be added back to the fruit.

❹ The poached fruit can be served straight away – it's lovely piled on top of a meringue, added to Greek yogurt, or served with whipped cream or ice cream.

❺ Keep refrigerated in sterilized jars (see p.222) for up to a week, or freeze in containers for up to 3 months.

Spicy Plum/ Damson Sauce

This sauce is lovely, either added to a stir-fry or used as a dipping sauce for chunks of meat, fish or steamed vegetables. It uses the syrup that you drained from the Poached Plums/Damsons recipe, on p51.

Makes 700ml (24fl oz/3 cups)

500ml (17fl oz/2 cups) Plum/Damson Syrup (see p51)

1–2 garlic cloves, finely sliced

1–2 small hot chillies, deseeded and finely chopped

4-cm (1-in) piece of fresh ginger, peeled and finely chopped

100ml (3½fl oz/generous ⅓ cup) soy sauce

100ml (3½fl oz/generous ⅓ cup) rice or cider vinegar

❶ Put all the ingredients in a saucepan, stir well and bring to the boil. Boil rapidly for 5 minutes, then remove from the heat and let cool a little.

❷ Pour the warm sauce into sterilized jars/bottles (see p.222). This will keep for a year in a cold larder or the refrigerator.

Since Plums, Damsons and Sloes generally appear in abundance, you will probably fill the entire freezer with them in no time! Luckily they all freeze very well, meaning that you can make this delicious (and nutritious) smoothie to keep you healthy even in the winter months. The oats are optional – they will make your smoothie thicker. Also, make sure that your mixture of fruits contains no more than 10–20% Sloes, as they can be quite acidic.

Serves 4

500g (18oz) mixture of frozen plums, damsons and sloes (maximum 20% sloes)

450g (1lb/4¾ cups) yogurt (either a plain one or your favourite fruity one)

150ml (5fl oz/⅔ cup) milk (any kind: cow's milk, oat milk, coconut milk, etc.)

20g (¾oz/3 tbsp) porridge (rolled) oats (optional)

1 tbsp maple syrup

squeeze of lemon juice

Plum Family Super Smoothie

❶ First, you will need to get the stones out of the fruit. When the fruit is frozen, this becomes much easier. Cut the fruit in half with a sharp knife and the stone will detach easily. The final weight of the stoned fruit will be about 450g (1lb).

❷ Simply put all the ingredients, except for the oats, into a blender and process until smooth. If you're using a hand-held (immersion) blender, put all the ingredients into a deep bowl before blending, so that the mixture can't splash everywhere. If you're using oats, stir them through at the end and leave the smoothie to stand for at least 20 minutes to soften. Drink immediately.

Elder
Sambucus nigra

Habitat: Country hedgerows and city parks/gardens

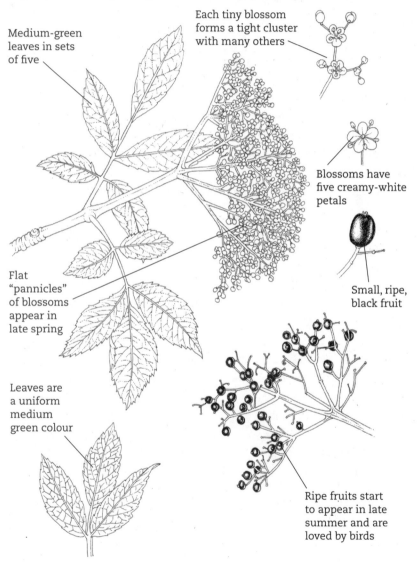

Medium-green leaves in sets of five

Each tiny blossom forms a tight cluster with many others

Blossoms have five creamy-white petals

Flat "pannicles" of blossoms appear in late spring

Small, ripe, black fruit

Leaves are a uniform medium green colour

Ripe fruits start to appear in late summer and are loved by birds

How can I recognize Elder and where can I find it?

In the winter, you'll see this rather straggly tree sprouting out of hedgerows, growing on wasteland, or popping up in gardens just where the gardener doesn't want it (some people don't realize their luck). Once the foliage begins to appear, though, the tree starts to look more interesting. It has grey/green leaves; an expert would describe these leaves as "pinnately divided into separate leaflets". All this means is that each leaf stem has smaller leaves (called "leaflets") set out in pairs (as though they were reflecting each other) along either side of the stem. These leaflets are oval-shaped with lightly serrated edges, a bit like little teeth. "Pinnate" means "feather-like", because the leaflets appear on both sides of the stem, in the same way that the tiny strands of a feather are laid along both sides of a central seam.

When the blossoms appear in late spring, the Elder tree is transformed into an explosion of frothy blossom.

Look at these more closely and you'll see that each bundle actually consists of zillions of tiny, creamy white blooms, each with speckles of bright yellow pollen dusting its interior. A few months later, in late summer and into early autumn (fall), each of those flowers will have transformed into a dark, blue-black berry.

If you fancy introducing Elder into your garden, cuttings will grow easily. Otherwise, the seeds tend to get spread by the animals who eat the berries. Nature runs its course, the seeds come out of the animal in the traditional way (think about it), and a new tree grows where they land.

All about Elder

The Elder is a very ancient tree indeed. We know that it has been present in northern Europe since before the last Ice Age (which finished, give or take a week or so, about 12,000 years ago). But its name has nothing to do with its great age. "Elder" is actually based on an Anglo-Saxon word – "aeld", meaning "fire". This is because the stems of the tree are easy to hollow out, and were used for making a tube which was handy to blow through to stir the sparks of a fire into flames without burning yourself. Even better, if you dried out the sticky pith that you poked out of the Elder stem, it would catch light very easily. If you want to think for a moment about just how useful this could be, imagine if you lived in a time without matches/lighters/flamethrowers or any of that sort of stuff. How would you go about making a fire?

What other things could you do with a hollow tube? How about using it as a pea shooter? This is the sort of thing that kids did in the days before electronic "devices". Get a packet of dried peas, pop one in the end of the Elder stem and blow it out with a determined blast of air. See who can get the pea to shoot the furthest distance.

Lots of plants have strange superstitions attached to them, and the Elder has more than most. Thinking about why these superstitions came about might give you an idea of how people used to think...

Here's a short list of a few of those old beliefs:

• The tree is inhabited by a spirit called The Elder Mother.
• If you cut the tree without asking permission, she'll get cross.
• If you have an Elder growing outside your door, you'll be protected from witches and other assorted evil spirits/entities/monsters/dragons/etc.
• Stand under the Elder tree at Midsummer and you'll see fairies.
• Fall asleep under the tree and the fairies will take you away.

Perhaps the idea of the "Elder Mother" was invented by someone so that the tree might be protected.

We tend to be superstitious about certain plants simply because they're so useful. We know that Elder is a helpful medicinal plant and so, in the days before we had chemists' shops on every corner, it would have made sense not to cut it down.

Also, both the blossoms and berries of this plant are not only edible but actually delicious. You might have heard of elderflower cordial? You can buy it in shops if you like, but if you make a simple elderflower syrup (see p.58), and dilute it to make a cordial, it will taste at least a million times better than anything in the shops. And it's MUCH cheaper, too.

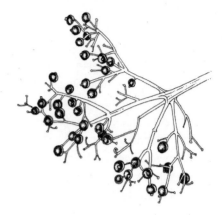

Harvesting Elder

Find a group of Elder trees, away from the road, which have low-hanging, easy-to-pick blossoms. You want to be able to reach the blossoms without the need for a chair or ladder. It's important not to collect all the blossoms you need from just one tree. Why not? Well, later in the year, the blossoms left on the tree will turn into berries. The berries are very valuable for boosting your immune system – if you make a

drink from them (see p.60), it will help keep you free of colds and flu all winter long (this has been proven in laboratories, by the way). Even more importantly, the berries are very useful autumn (fall) food for birds and animals – and, let's face it, they were here before us. They need all the help they can get in the run-up to winter (see Rules of Foraging Number 1: Don't Be Greedy).

• Collect the blossoms when the heat of the sun is on them – they must be dry. The bunches should snap easily away from the stem.
• Make sure each panicle of blossoms doesn't have any brown bits and smells gorgeous. If elderflower blossoms are "on the turn" (that's what my Gran used to say when she meant "going off" or "over-ripe"), then the resulting

syrup will taste a bit weird (apparently like cat pee, not that I have ever actually tasted that!).

• Don't wash the blossoms. The lovely scent and flavour of elderflower is held in the pollen. If you wash the flowers, you will wash away much of the flavour.

• Use them straight away. If you can't do this, keep them in a cool place and use as soon as possible. After two days, they will be no good.

• To allow any bugs to leave the flowers, turn your container of blossoms upside-down on a sheet of newspaper, preferably on a table outside. Prop up one side of the container with something – a brick or rock will do fine. The bugs won't like being in the dark and will simply leave via the "door" you've made. Leave for a couple of hours for the insects to leave and go back to their work and families.

A NOTE OF CAUTION: on rare occasions, some people can get an upset tummy if they eat too many raw elderberries. Boiling the berries for a short time solves this problem.

The Best Elderflower Syrup Recipe in the World

This recipe might seem to have a lot of instructions, but don't worry. Wild ingredients are not like something you'd buy in a supermarket; they have a different set of rules and it is important to treat them in the right way.

This is the best elderflower syrup recipe you'll find anywhere. It's easy to get right and, although you more usually see recipes for elderflower cordial, I'm giving you a more versatile syrup here. Syrup is more concentrated than cordial and you can do lots of other things with it: it can be poured over ice cream; made into lollipops or jelly; you can even make a delicious sorbet by semi-freezing, mashing with a fork, and freezing again. If you want to drink it as a cordial, simply dilute to taste with still or sparkling water.

Makes 1l (35fl oz/4¼ cups)

500ml (17fl oz/generous 2 cups) boiling
    water
450g (1lb/2¼ cups) white organic caster
    (superfine) sugar
2 unwaxed lemons, cut into quarters
20–30 elderflower heads, picked and
    de-bugged (see p.58)

❶ Put the boiling water and sugar into a large saucepan or bowl. Squeeze and squash the lemon quarters over the pan and drop them in too. Stir to dissolve the sugar, and leave until cool.

❷ Meanwhile, pick your elderflowers, lay them out on sheets on newspaper and debug them (see p.58).

❸ When the sugar syrup mixture is cold, add the flowers to the syrup, removing the blossoms from the stalks with your fingers. A few bits of stalk will always end up in the mix, but don't worry. Carefully lift the newspaper that the flowers have been sitting on (this will have lots of tasty pollen on it), fold the paper in half and brush the extra pollen into the water. (This little tip, I am sure, is why this recipe is so good. I don't know of anyone else that does this, so please keep it a secret.)

Cover the pan/bowl with a clean dish towel or some foil and leave in a cool place for 2 days, stirring occasionally. After 2 days, taste the syrup – if you feel you could leave it a little longer, do so.

❹ Line a fine-mesh sieve (strainer) with a piece of clean muslin (cheesecloth) and set it over another large, clean bowl. Pour the mixture into the lined sieve and let the liquid drip slowly into the bowl. Once all the liquid has dripped through, transfer it to a large clean jug (pitcher) and use a funnel to pour the syrup into sterilized containers (see p.222) – 500ml (17 fl oz) bottles are good. Seal with a lid and keep in the refrigerator for 3–4 weeks. If you want to freeze the syrup, leave 4cm (1½in) empty at the top of each bottle to allow room for the frozen syrup to expand. It will keep indefinitely in the freezer and can even be thawed and re-frozen.

❺ The leftover elderflowers and lemons can be put on the compost heap or into the food recycling bin.

Spiced Elderberry Syrup

Medical science has proven that Elderberries have an anti-viral effect, proving the ancient people who used them to stay well in the winter months were right! This recipe is not only simple and good for you, but also tastes delicious!

Makes 750ml (26fl oz/3¼ cups)

at least 20 bunches of elderberries, stripped from the stalks
juice of 1 orange
juice of 1 lemon
250g (9oz/1¼ cups) sugar of your choice (or honey, if preferred)
1 cinnamon stick
4-cm (1½-in) piece of fresh ginger
a few cloves
1 star anise (optional)
1 green cardamom pod (optional)

❶ Put the berries into a heavy pan with a lid, add the orange and lemon juice, and then add enough water to cover the berries by about 3cm (1in). Add all the rest of the ingredients.

❷ Bring to the boil, cover, and let boil for 2 minutes. Lower the heat, remove the lid, then simmer for a further 15–20 minutes. Set aside until completely cool.

❸ Strain the liquid through a fine-mesh sieve (strainer) into a bowl or jug, removing any solid pieces of ginger or spices (these can be reused in a chutney or relish, or even frozen to add to your bird table in the winter!).

❹ Allow the liquid to drip through the sieve until you don't think there's any more left, then press down on the pulp with a spoon... there will be more!

❺ Use a funnel and ladle to decant the liquid into sterilized 500ml (17fl oz) bottles (see p.222), leaving a little space at the top for expansion if freezing. It can also be put into ice-cube trays, so that you only need to defrost a little at a time. Freeze until needed, or it will keep in the refrigerator for up to 6 months.

❻ This elderberry syrup is lovely poured over ice cream, stirred into porridge or mixed with hot water to make a delicious drink. I'm sure you'll think of lots of ways of using it.

Hawthorn
Crataegus monogyna

Habitat: Hedgerows

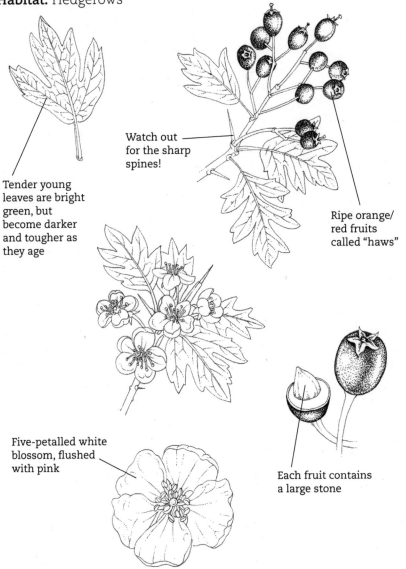

Tender young leaves are bright green, but become darker and tougher as they age

Watch out for the sharp spines!

Ripe orange/ red fruits called "haws"

Five-petalled white blossom, flushed with pink

Each fruit contains a large stone

There are lots of different names for this plant, including Whitethorn, Maythorn, May Blossom and May Tree. One of the more unusual names, and one that might be rather puzzling, is "Bread and Cheese" or "Bread and Honey". This is because, not so very long ago, children walking to school would munch on the fresh young leaves. Ask older people if they remember doing this. The leaves are actually quite nice when young, and make a good fresh green addition to a salad or sandwich. Don't bother trying them once they turn a darker green, because they get very tough and leathery.

The flowers of the Hawthorn are also edible; pick off the individual blossoms and add them to a salad.

Hawthorn can grow to quite a great age. You might have heard of the Glastonbury Thorn, a Hawthorn tree with legendary status (a legend is an old story which may or may not be true). The story goes that this particular Hawthorn tree grew from a branch that was thrust into the ground at Glastonbury in Somerset, in the UK, by Joseph of Arimathea (a character swathed in legends, said to be a disciple of Christ, and alive at the same time). Joseph of Arimethea is rumoured to have visited Britain to tell people about Jesus. We are unlikely to find out whether or not any of this is true. We do know, though, that the Glastonbury Thorn was first mentioned in the 16th century, which would make it at least 400 years old. Sadly, the tree was vandalized in 2010, but this unfortunate incident is not the first time that the tree has suffered; people have been taking cuttings from it for centuries. Maybe this "pruning" has strengthened the tree.

The shiny red berries of the hawthorn are called "haws". This word originally meant "hedge", and describes the use to which this plant has been put for thousands of years – as boundary hedging.

The fact that it grows quickly, is impenetrable and also has sharp spines, means that is makes the perfect barrier to keep animals safe from harm (and also to keep them from eating valuable crops).

How can I recognize Hawthorn and where can I find it?

Hawthorn is often used for hedging, and so is often cut back, but when left to grow unchecked this plant can reach up to 15m (49ft) tall. Hawthorn tends to be quite an untidy-looking shrub/tree, with tangled branches and long thorns. In the summer months, it is covered in creamy-white frothy blossoms, clustered in groups, with five petals per flower. The leaves are quite distinctive – about 6cm (2½in) long, with deeply cut "lobes" or "tongues". The younger leaves are pale green, darkening in colour and becoming quite leathery and tough with age. The timber of the tree is very strong; the name "Crataegus" means "strong" and "sharp". Hawthorn wood has been used for centuries by carpenters and wood-turners to make parts for boats, as well as boxes and handles for furniture.

You'll see Hawthorn most commonly in hedgerows in rural areas, as well as in city gardens and parks. It often grows alongside the Blackthorn (p.44), whose flowers appear prior to the leaves. The Hawthorn works the other way round – its leaves appear before the white flowers.

Spicy Hawthorn Relish

This is a really good dip for nachos and also makes an interesting substitute for tomato ketchup! If you are not a fan of spice, you can omit the chilli!

Makes 2 x 300-g (10½-oz) jars

1kg (35oz) fresh haws, stalks removed, washed and patted dry

500ml (17fl oz/2 cups) apple cider vinegar

300g (10½oz/1½ cups) brown sugar

150g (5½oz/1 cup) cherry tomatoes, slit with a knife

1 medium red chilli, finely chopped (including seeds)

3 garlic cloves, crushed

1 tsp ground ginger

½ tsp ground nutmeg

¼ tsp ground cloves

¼ tsp allspice

freshly ground black pepper, to taste

❶ Put the washed haws into a large, heavy pan with a lid and cover with water. Put the lid on the pan, bring to the boil and simmer for 30 minutes, until the haws are soft.

❷ Allow to cool, then strain through a sieve (strainer) set over a bowl to remove all the stones.

❸ Put the haw pulp back into the pan with all the other ingredients. Bring to a simmer and cook for 30 minutes, uncovered, stirring from time to time, until the mixture has reduced a little.

❹ Let the relish cool for a few minutes, then pour into warm sterilized jars (see p.222). It will keep for at least a month in the refrigerator, but tastes better if brought to room temperature before eating.

Rowan

Sorbus aucuparia

Habitat: Rocky, hilly places with a slightly acidic soil, street plantings, gardens

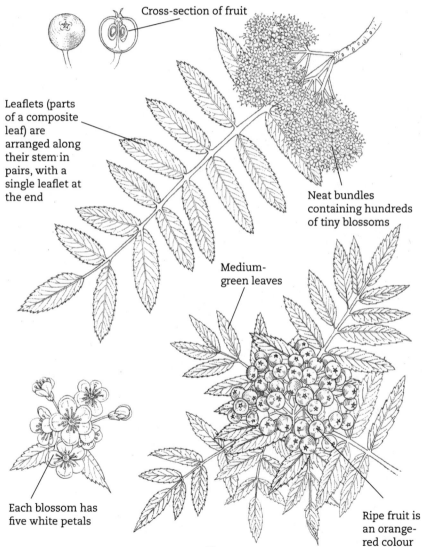

Cross-section of fruit

Leaflets (parts of a composite leaf) are arranged along their stem in pairs, with a single leaflet at the end

Neat bundles containing hundreds of tiny blossoms

Medium-green leaves

Each blossom has five white petals

Ripe fruit is an orange-red colour

Rowan trees grow wild in hilly places. One of its folk names is Mountain Ash, not only because it will grow at altitude but also because the leaves resemble those of the Ash tree. It's a very useful tree for many different caterpillars, such as the Emperor Moth and Apple Fruit Moth, who feed on the leaves. Birds that enjoy the red berries include Blackbirds and Mistle Thrushes.

As with many trees, there are some interesting superstitions about the Rowan. For example, back when people thought that witches were real, they believed that the tree would protect them. It was sometimes called the Witch Wiggin Tree. Do you believe that a tree could have this sort of power? Why do you think people from times gone by, who may not have been educated, had such superstitions?

How can I recognize Rowan and where can I find it?

The Rowan is a very pretty tree, growing to a height of 15–20m (49–65ft) tall. It has been known to reach the grand age of 200 years. It grows wild in cooler climates and high altitude, but is

> ### Names around the world
>
> **French** Sorbier
> **German** Eberesche
> **Spanish** Serbal
> **Welsh** Criafol
> **Polish** Jarząb pospolity, Jarzębina
> **Swedish** Rönn
>
> **Your name for this plant:**
>
> ....

quite common in urban areas and gardens as well.

The leaves of the Rowan grow to approximately 16cm (6¼in) in length, with five to eight pairs of leaflets running down each side of a stem; they are very similar to those of Roses (p.68). In the spring, the leaves start to appear, followed by the flower buds, which are ball-like clusters of creamy white fluffy bundles, dotted around the tree. After the flowers, come the berries. When ripe, these orange-red bundles of pea-sized fruits make it easy to spot the tree from a distance. As the autumn (fall) months lengthen into winter, the leaves of the Rowan turn to red, and fall to the ground.

This recipe works well since both apples and Rowan berries are in season at the same time. Also, the natural pectin in the apples helps the jelly to set. If you don't have any rose petals, or don't want to use them, simply leave them out.

Rowan, Apple and Rose Jelly

Makes 4 x 300-g (10½-oz) jars

2kg (4½lb) rowan berries, destalked and washed

1.5kg (3½lb) apples (any kind), cut into 2-cm (¾-in) chunks

handful of strongly-scented rose petals (optional)

granulated sugar, see method for quantity

1 Put the berries and apples into a large saucepan and cover with water. Cover and set over a medium-low heat. Allow to simmer for up to 40 minutes, until squishy. Set aside till just warm, then add the rose petals (if using).

2 Let the mixture cool, then set up a jelly bag with a tripod (a muslin/cheesecloth or clean linen dish towel set over a colander works as well) over a large bowl. Pour the mixture into the bag and let it drip overnight. Don't squeeze the liquid through the bag, as this will make your jelly look cloudy.

3 Measure the liquid collected by pouring it into a measuring jug, then measure out the same volume of sugar (500g/18oz/2½ cups sugar to 600ml/20fl oz/2½ cups liquid).

4 Put the liquid and sugar in the saucepan, set over a medium-low heat and stir gently until the sugar has dissolved. Then turn up the heat and bring the liquid to boiling point. Boil until a few drops dripped onto an ice-cold saucer will wrinkle when pressed with a finger. Pour into warm, sterilized jars (see p.222) and seal.

5 If scum settles on top of the liquid during cooking, skim away with a spoon. If you prefer not to waste your foraged ingredients, you can spread it on toast (there's nothing wrong with it – it just looks a bit weird!). Rowan jelly will keep indefinitely if unopened. Once opened, refrigerate and use within 2 weeks.

Rose

Rosa

Habitat: Anywhere and everywhere, although the richer the soil, the more prolific the roses

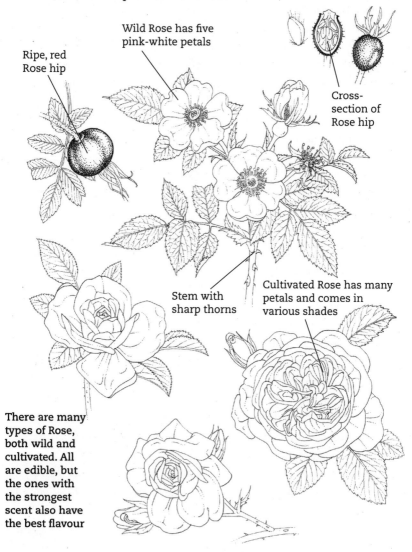

Wild Rose has five pink-white petals

Ripe, red Rose hip

Cross-section of Rose hip

Stem with sharp thorns

Cultivated Rose has many petals and comes in various shades

There are many types of Rose, both wild and cultivated. All are edible, but the ones with the strongest scent also have the best flavour

Roses grow all over the planet, and there is probably no other flower which is loved so much, or which means so much, to so many people.

The eagle-eyed amongst you will notice how incredibly similar are all the different names for the Rose in the different languages, above. There are several hundred different varieties of Roses. As well as the wild types (which include Rosa canina, Rosa virginiana and Rosa acicularis) there are hundreds of different sorts of Roses that have been cultivated and hybridized (this means "mixed together") to make even more varieties.

It is likely that these lovely flowers first appeared in Persia (a country now called Iran), from where they spread around the rest of the world.

How can I recognize Roses and where can I find them?

Wild Roses (Rosa canina, for example, which means "dog rose") frequently grow in older hedgerows, where they scramble

---

Names around the world

French Roses, Rosiers

German Rosen

Spanish Rosas

Welsh Rhosynnau

Polish Róże

Swedish Ros

Your name for this plant:

....

---

through other plants. They have long, slim, prickly branches, which often arch up through the greenery of the other plants. In the summer months these Wild Roses bear very pretty pink-white flowers, with five petals. Some time after the petals have fallen, a small, bright red "berry" appears; this is the fruit of the Rose, which is called a "Rose hip".

The much-loved kinds of Roses that grow in gardens are larger and showier than the wild ones. They have many more petals, too, and larger, more bulbous hips.

Serving suggestions

When I'm leading foraging walks, one of the most frequently asked questions is this:

"Is it possible to eat Wild Roses, as well as "tame" ones?" The answer is a big, fat YES! You can eat any Rose, so long as it hasn't been sprayed with insecticides or other chemicals.

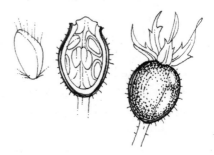

You can eat the petals, and the Rose hips, and even the leaves. The petals won't taste of very much unless they have a strong scent. Always try the sniff test first with Rose petals!

Rose hips have to be processed before using. If you cut one open, you will see lots of tiny, hairy seeds – these can be very irritating to your throat if you swallow them, and can also irritate your skin (sometimes they are used as itching powder), so the seeds need to be removed. I'll tell you how to do this later.

Over the next few pages are three recipes, each using different parts of the Rose.

This recipe is so simple! Make sure that you pick Rose leaves that are perfect, with no black spots or mould on them.

Makes enough for 10 cups of tea

1 large handful rose leaves

milk, to taste (optional)

sugar, to taste (optional)

slice of lemon (optional)

Rose Leaf Tea

1 Remove the rose leaves from their stems and discard the stems.

2 Spread the leaves out on a sheet of white paper, making sure that none of the leaves are touching each other (otherwise they can get mildew). Leave for 2 weeks in a cool, dry atmosphere.

3 By this time the leaves will have turned a dark green/black colour. Gather the leaves up and crumble them; they should crumble easily between your fingertips. They will look like tea leaves. Store them in an airtight container.

4 Use the crumbled leaves exactly as you would use loose-leaf tea. Warm a teapot by swirling hot water around inside it, then pour out. Add 1 level teaspoon of crumbled rose leaves per cup into the teapot, then pour over boiling water. Leave to steep for a good 5 minutes. You can add milk and sugar to taste, if you wish. I prefer rose-leaf tea with just a slice of lemon.

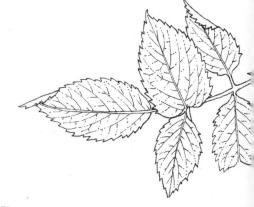

Rose Hip Syrup

Traditionally, this syrup was used because of its vitamin C content. In the UK, just after the end of the Second World War, school children were sent out to pick rose hips, and the resulting syrup was given to young mothers to give them some extra nutrition.

There are lots of ways to use it: you can dilute it in hot or cold water, as a cordial; pour it over porridge in the winter, or over ice cream in the summer. You can also make a sorbet from it. Pour it into a tub with a lid, then put into the freezer for an hour or so. Take the tub out of the freezer, mash up the ice crystals with a fork, then freeze again, until just soft enough to spoon into dishes.

Makes about 1l (35fl oz/4¼ cups)

1kg (35oz) rose hips, washed and
  picked over for leaves and bits
  of stick
450g (1lb/2¼ cups) granulated sugar
juice of 4 lemons

❶ Put 1.7l (60fl oz/7½ cups) of water into a large saucepan and bring to the boil.

❷ Meanwhile, mash the rose hips a little with a potato masher.

❸ Once the water is boiling, add the rose hips and bring back to the boil. Boil for 3 minutes, then remove the pan from the heat and leave for 30 minutes to cool.

❹ Once cool, sieve the mixture through a fine-mesh sieve (strainer) into a large bowl. Rinse the pan and set aside.

❺ Set up a jelly bag with a tripod (a muslin/cheesecloth or clean linen dish towel set over a colander works as well) over a bowl and strain the mixture again, to ensure that all the little hairs from the seeds are removed. Return the sieved liquid to the pan, and add the sugar and 800ml (28fl oz/scant 3½ cups) water. Boil until the liquid has reduced by approximately one quarter. Allow to cool, then add the lemon juice. Leave to cool completely.

❻ Store your syrup in sterilized jars or bottles (see p.222), leaving space in the top of the bottles for the liquid to expand if you want to freeze it. It will keep for a month in the refrigerator, or indefinitely in the freezer.

Rose Petal Sandwiches

This is a very old-fashioned recipe, dating back to at least 1900, which I found tucked into the pages of an old cookery book that I bought in a second-hand bookshop. That was a lucky day!

Makes 2 "normal" sandwiches or 16 small "finger" sandwiches

4–5 handfuls of strongly-scented pink or red rose petals

115g (4oz/½ cup) unsalted butter, chopped into thin slices (about 4mm/⅛in)

4 slices of bread

granulated sugar, for sprinkling

❶ Cover the bottom of a dish with a layer of dry, unblemished, strongly-scented rose petals.

❷ Lay the slices of butter on top of the rose petals, then take more petals and completely cover the butter with them. Cover with clingfilm (plastic wrap) and leave in a cool place overnight.

❸ The next day, remove the petals and set aside. Thinly spread the butter (which will have absorbed the flavour of the roses) over the bread slices. Add a layer of petals to 2 of the slices and a sprinkling of sugar, then top with the other 2 slices of bread. Cut into two, or cut into smaller "finger" sandwiches, if you prefer. The perfect party treat!

WILD
HERBS
& WEEDS

About Herbs & Weeds

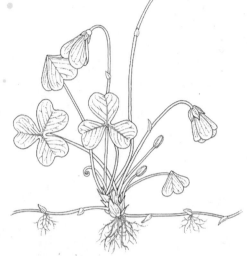

Let's clear up what I mean by weeds! When my editor suggested that one of the plant categories might include "weeds", I was astounded. As far as I'm concerned, there's no such thing as a weed. But I thought about the suggestion and decided to include it, mainly so that I can tell you what, exactly, is meant by a "weed".

Some people will tell you that a weed is just "a plant that's in the wrong place" or "a plant that's growing where you don't want it". This is quite a common definition. However, ask yourself this: does the "weed" think that it is in the wrong place? Does the "weed" think that it is unwanted? Unless you're able to speak "plant", then you'll never know the answer.

Let's consider the plants that people think are weeds. Dandelions? Nettles? Daisies? Even "wild herbs", to those who don't know about them, can also come under the weed category. Once you start to learn a little about these plants, and how useful they are in all sorts of ways, you will find that the word "weed" becomes less and less appropriate and more and more insulting. Many people call plants weeds because they don't know them. They don't know the name, or anything about the plant, even though they may pass by it nearly every single day. Take Ground Elder, for example. Many gardeners spend lots of money (and time) trying to eradicate it from their gardens. However, once they're properly introduced to it, those with an imagination will suddenly realize that they have a crop to be treasured rather than a weed to be hated. Some of the weeds that are most common are plants that once had a great deal of value or were in everyday use; Pineapple Weed is one of these, as are Hairy Bittercress and Nettles.

The plants that we call weeds are among the toughest and most resilient of all – the ones that refuse to go away!

Here's an idea that might make you think: when we say that a person is "weedy", we mean that they are feeble and weak. And yet the plants that we call weeds are among the toughest and most resilient of all – the ones that refuse to go away! So really, when we call someone "weedy", it should actually be a compliment!

As a forager, it is part of your job to help people understand just how powerful and useful plants can be for human beings. It is your mission to tell people, very kindly and without making them seem stupid, the name of the plant and also a little bit about it. Even this small act can make people think again and look at the world in a much more sensible way.

"Weeds" indeed!

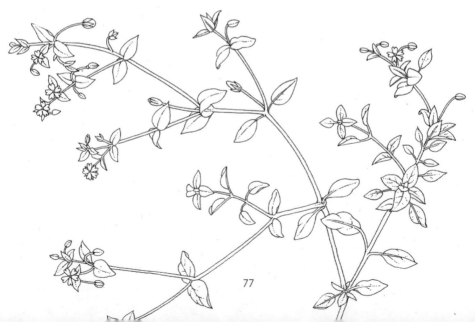

Burdock

Arctium lappa

Habitat: Wasteland, edges of woodland, scrubland

The "burrs" are green-purple, prickly and fuzzy

Large, floppy leaf. In its first year of growth it is close to the ground and looks like a large dock leaf

Erect stems

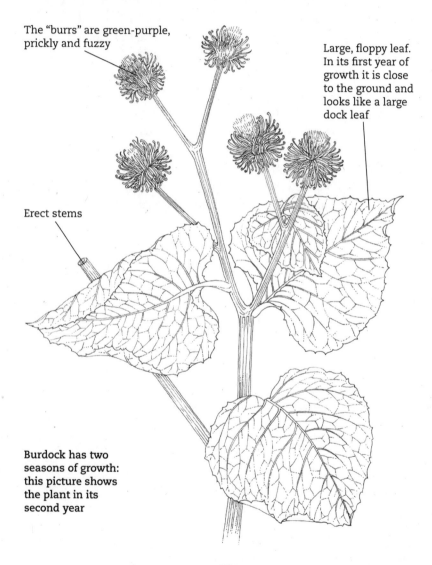

Burdock has two seasons of growth: this picture shows the plant in its second year

The Latin names of this plant mean "bear" and "rough", and the fuzzy, prickly burrs, which are the flowers of Burdock, do look a bit bear-like. Burdock is one of the many plants that was once highly regarded, but which seems to have fallen out of fashion (in some countries) of late. The long tap root is the part of the plant that is used. Burdock root has a satisfyingly crunchy texture and an unusual flavour. At first, it can taste quite earthy, then it becomes sweeter, a bit like carrots or parsnips, with an undercurrent of artichoke. In upmarket farmers' markets, you might see the long, thin roots sold as "Niu Bang"(the Chinese name) or "Gobo" (its name in Japan). When sold in this way, Burdock roots can be quite expensive. It is this same root that you can dig up and eat for free.

How can I recognize Burdock and where can I find it?

Often mistaken for dock leaves, young Burdock leaves are a darker green and thicker in texture; they become much bigger, too, stretching to a magnificent 1m (3ft) wide and a little more in length. In its first year of growth,

Names around the world	
French	Bardane
German	Grosse klette ("large fastener" – find out why later!)
Spanish	Bardana
Welsh	Caci mwnci
Polish	Łopian większy
Swedish	Stor kardborre
Japanese	Gobo
Chinese	Niu Bang

Your name for this plant:

....

you'll recognize Burdock by its large, heart-shaped leaves with wavy edges, which are green on the top and a pale greenish-white on the underside. Distinctively, at this point the Burdock has no stem. In its second year of growth, the plant gets both bushier and taller – up to 2m (6ft) – and develops stems that bear the prickly, fuzzy burrs that give the plant its name. These burrs are purple in colour, approximately 3cm (1¼in) in diameter and very prickly indeed, containing lots of tiny hooks that attach themselves to the backs of animals such as dogs, foxes and horses – oh, and people wearing woolly jumpers.

Burdock prefers full sun and grows on wasteland, at the edges of woods, in gardens, in city parks, and on riversides. Butterflies, bees and other insects feed on it, as do Goldfinches. If you're sharp-eyed, you might be lucky enough to see these tiny birds perched on the burrs, feasting on the seeds.

Serving suggestions

The best way to harvest Burdock roots without breaking them too much is to first choose a wet day, so the soil will be easier to break up, and then to dig a trench around the plant so that you can access the root more easily. The roots should be harvested in the autumn (fall) of the first year of growth – that is, before the distinctive burrs have appeared. At first, the roots are white; on exposure to the air, they turn yellow.

Wash the root, then peel away the bitter rind. Grate, and soak in water for 20 minutes or so. Drain well, then fry for 10–15 minutes, together with a little garlic, ginger and soy sauce. Alternatively, try my recipe on p.81.

DID YOU KNOW...
Do you have any clothes or bags which fasten with Velcro®? Here's how it was invented!

In the 1940s, a Swiss inventor and engineer called George de Mestral noticed, after taking his dog for a walk, that both his trousers and his pet were covered in the burrs of the Burdock plant. Inquisitive George had a close look at them under a microscope. What he saw fascinated him. There were lots of tiny hooks, used by the seeds to spread themselves by attaching themselves to passing animals. George realized that the same idea might be used to connect other things, too, and, in 1955 he revealed his invention to the world. Trying to think of a name, he came up with a combination of "velour" (meaning "velvet") and "crochet" (meaning "hook"). And that's how Velcro® came to be!

The invention was adopted by NASA and even reached the moon as part of the uniforms worn by the astronauts. It is strange to think that it was inspired by the annoying burrs of a plant that many consider to be a useless weed!

Have you heard of the fizzy drink called Dandelion and Burdock? Originally a cough medicine made from the roots of (surprise, surprise) Dandelion and Burdock plants, when sugar was added to the mixture it transformed into a delicious fizzy drink. It is still available, although most of the bottles that are sold today are made with artificial flavourings.

The good news is that you can make your own Dandelion and Burdock drink, which will be far superior to anything you'll find in the shops! For this, you will need to dry out the roots of both Burdock and Dandelion (see p.92). Then, you'll need to grind them – a coffee grinder is best, otherwise use a food processor.

Makes 700–800ml (24–28fl oz/ 3–3½ cups)

1l (35fl oz/4¼ cups) water
1½ tsp each ground burdock root and ground dandelion root (see above and p.95)
2-cm (¾-in) piece of fresh ginger
1 whole star anise or 2 green cardamom pods, crushed
350g (12oz/scant 1¾ cups) caster (superfine) sugar
sparkling water and ice, to serve

Dandelion and Burdock Drink

❶ Put all the ingredients, except for the sugar and sparkling water, into a heavy saucepan, bring to the boil, then reduce the heat, cover, and simmer for 25–30 minutes.

❷ Let cool, then strain into a bowl, using a fine-mesh sieve (strainer) lined with muslin (cheesecloth) to make sure no little bits manage to escape.

❸ Rinse the pan, return the liquid to it and set over a low heat. Add the sugar, and warm through until melted. Set aside until cold.

❹ Dilute the syrup to taste with sparkling water, stir well and serve over ice.

❺ Pour into sterilized bottles (see p.222) and store in the refrigerator for up to 2 weeks. Alternatively freeze (leave space at the top of the bottles for the liquid to expand as it freezes) and defrost as needed.

Chickweed

Stellaria media

Habitat: Gardens, verges, edge places

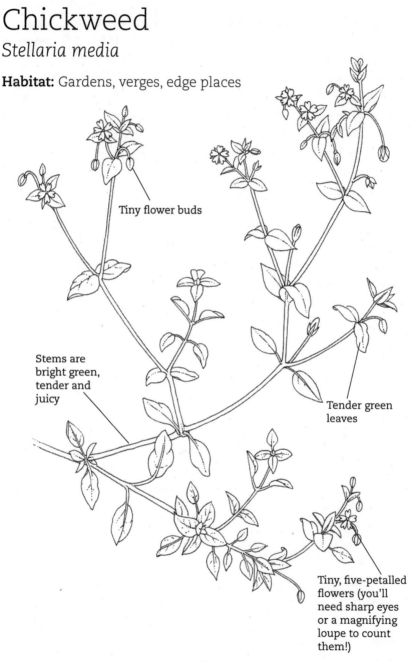

Tiny flower buds

Stems are bright green, tender and juicy

Tender green leaves

Tiny, five-petalled flowers (you'll need sharp eyes or a magnifying loupe to count them!)

How can I recognize Chickweed and where can I find it?

As you might imagine from the name, chickens love eating Chickweed! And they're right to do so. This is a pretty little plant, sometimes called "common chickweed" to differentiate it from other plants that are also called chickweed. It is often overlooked or ignored, since many people don't realize how flavoursome it is. Chickweed likes growing in the shady ground under large oak or beech trees, where its splash of bright green can be seen clearly in the gloomy shadows. It is also commonly found in gardens, on verges and at the edges of grain fields.

Chickweed is a tender, rather fragile-looking plant, with tiny, white, star-shaped flowers, that are visible in the summer months. Each of these flowers has what initially appears to be ten white petals, but if you look closely you'll see that there are actually just five petals, each almost forked in half. These star-shaped flowers are what gives the plant the "stellaria" part of its name; "media" means "medium" or "between".

Where it is left to its own devices, Chickweed can grow long, sprawling stems which form dense green mats. These mats can be found at all times of the year, even in the depths of winter.

As a vegetable, Chickweed is tender, succulent and, above all, tasty. This, combined with its year-round availability, makes this plant a very useful one to find. Since it is so tender, heating it up is a waste of time. Try it in a salad, or make yourself an Egg and Chickweed Sandwich (see p.84). Delicious!

Names around the world

French	Mouron blanc (Mouron des oiseaux)
German	Acker hornkraut
Spanish	Alsine o hierba gallinera
Welsh	Gwlyddyn
Polish	Gwiazdnica pospolita
Swedish	Våtarv

Your name for this plant:

....

Egg and Chickweed Sandwiches

This is a simple but tasty sandwich. You can also use Chickweed to make a pesto, added to other leaves such as Wild Garlic, Ground Elder or Jack-by-the-Hedge (see p.179 for how to make pesto).

Serves 1

1 egg

a dash of vinegar

a dollop of mayonnaise (optional)

a handful of freshly picked chickweed, washed and patted dry

2 slices of bread

butter

salt and freshly ground black pepper

❶ Put the egg into a small saucepan of cold water, making sure there's enough water to cover the egg. Add a dash of vinegar. Bring the water to the boil, and boil the egg for 5 minutes (so that it is hard boiled).

❷ Turn off the heat and use a slotted spoon to transfer the cooked egg to a bowl of cold water to cool it down. When cool enough to handle, dry the egg with a paper towel, then crack and peel the shell off. Put the peeled egg in a bowl and mash with a fork, adding a dollop of mayonnaise if you like.

❸ Fold in the fresh chickweed and sprinkle with salt and pepper to taste.

❹ Butter the bread, then spoon the egg and chickweed mixture onto one slice. Pop the second slice on top and cut in half. Eat!

Cleavers
Galium aparine

Habitat: Anywhere and everywhere, but prefers damp shade rather than full sun

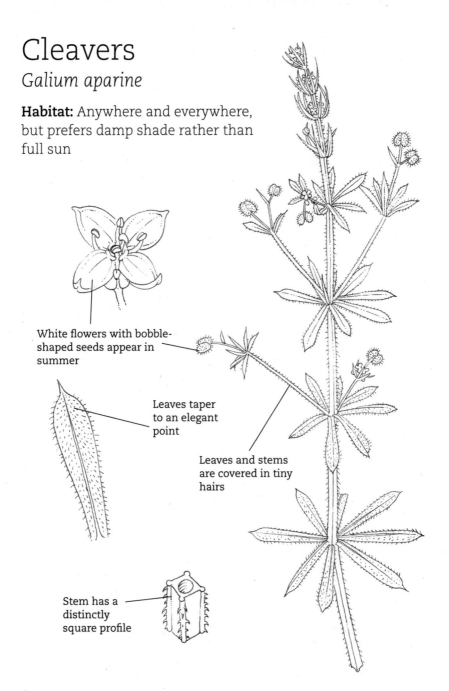

White flowers with bobble-shaped seeds appear in summer

Leaves taper to an elegant point

Leaves and stems are covered in tiny hairs

Stem has a distinctly square profile

If you've never heard of Cleavers before, and this book introduces you to them, then this one small plant means that the entire book has been worthwhile!

The name "Galium" is from the Greek word "gala", meaning "milk". At one time, the plant was used to curdle milk in the process of making cheese. The "aparine" part of the name also is of Greek origin; it means to "take hold of". The definitive quality of this plant is its fuzzy stickiness, which has triggered lots of different names, all with a similar theme. To "cleave" means to hold onto something. Other names include Sticky Grass, Sticky Willy, Sticky Bobs, and Stickleback. It's also sometimes referred to as Goosegrass, as it has been used as a food for geese, who love it, for many generations. Chickens love it too.

It's not only good food for birds! We humans can eat Cleavers too. This plant is actually related to coffee, and the seeds can be gathered, dried and roasted to make a coffee-like drink.

Names around the world

French	Gaillet Gratteron
German	Labkräuter
Spanish	Amor de hortelano
Welsh	Gwlydd y perthi
Polish	Przytulia czepna
Swedish	Snärjmåra

Your name for this plant:

....

Matted together, dried Cleavers were once used to stuff mattresses and pillows. In some parts of the world, the stems are woven into mats to make a sort of sieve for straining liquids. If you have a pond, you might have noticed that the surface of the water often gets covered in a thick layer of pond weed. Long bundles of Cleavers, clumped together and floated on the surface of the pond, will make removal of the pond weed to reveal clear water, a much easier task.

How can I recognize Cleavers and where can I find them?

The stem of this plant can grow up to 2m (6½ft) high in one season. Whorls of six–eight leaves

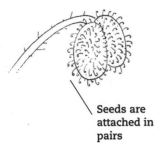

Seeds are attached in pairs

are spaced at regular intervals along those long stems (which are easy to break since they're not at all strong). Side shoots, also containing whorls of leaves, emerge where the leaves connect with the stem. The entire plant is covered with tiny little hooks that give it a fuzzy texture – it will stick to just about anything: fences, trees, walls, the fabric of your clothes, or the fur of animals!

In late spring and early summer, small white flowers appear at the tips of the stems. These flowers turn to small fuzzy bobbles, in groups of two or three, which are also very sticky and apt to cling to your clothes even more tenaciously than the stems.

You can find Cleavers just about anywhere, scrambling through hedgerows, or growing in dense mats over fences and garden walls.

It seems to take a perverse pleasure in invading gardens, to the annoyance of most gardeners who might not realize how useful it is. As well as growing upwards, Cleavers can also creep along the ground. It prefers places that are a bit shady and damp, rather than sunny and dry.

Serving suggestions

Like many other leafy vegetables, Cleavers are at their best to eat raw in the early spring months. Later on, the plant gets a bit tougher, but it is still good as a steamed vegetable. The recipe on p.88 uses the stalks and leaves of the Cleavers to add taste and texture to an omelette.

Cleavers Omelette

An omelette is not only simple to make, it is also delicious and nutritious. This recipe should make a perfect one every time.

Serves 1–2

2 large free-range eggs (even the best eggs are cheap, so don't make the mistake of buying ultra-cheap battery-farmed eggs)

1 tsp cold milk

1 small handful fresh cleavers, washed, patted dry and torn into small pieces

knob of butter

dash of oil

salt and freshly ground black pepper

❶ Crack the eggs into a mixing bowl, add the milk and a pinch each of salt and pepper, then whisk with a fork until very well blended. Stir in the cleavers.

❷ Melt the oil and butter together in a heavy frying pan (skillet) over a low heat. Turn the heat up and quickly pour in the egg mixture, swooshing it gently around in the pan so that the mixture is evenly spread over the base. Cook for 3 minutes, then use a spatula to lift the edge of the omelette and carefully fold it in half. Cook for another 1 minute, then carefully turn it with the spatula and cook the other side for about 1 minute, or until pale golden brown, then slide the omelette onto a warmed plate and serve.

❸ This is lovely served with a crisp green salad and a dash of chilli oil! You could cut it in half and share with a friend, or eat it all by yourself.

Daisy
Bellis perennis

Habitat: Open grasslands

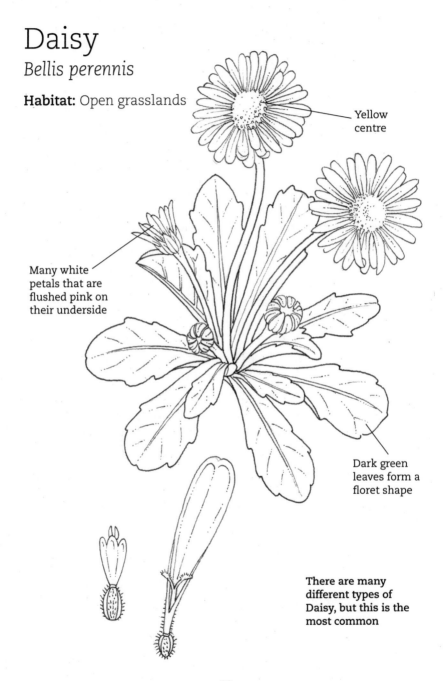

Yellow centre

Many white petals that are flushed pink on their underside

Dark green leaves form a floret shape

There are many different types of Daisy, but this is the most common

This entry refers to the Common Daisy, the small flower with a yellow centre and white petals that grows in open grassland. The botanical name means "beautiful perennial". A perennial is a plant that appears in the same place year after year. (An "annual" plant is one that flowers once, but seeds itself to make new flowers.)

Have you ever noticed that the petals of Daisies close up when it starts to get dark or cold?

They're not the only flower that does this, but it is this habit which gives this small flower it's name: "day's eye", and the literal Welsh translation, meaning "eye of the day".

The plant is also sometimes called "Bairnwort" ("bairn" is an old Scottish word meaning a young child), because children make them into Daisy chains. The Daisy was also called "Bruisewort", since it was used to soothe the pain of a bruise. More about that later!

I like the name in Swedish, which means "thousand beauties". Henrik, who translated the Swedish words for me, told me that his father would walk into expensive florists' shops and ask for a bunch of "Tusenskōna" since he thought they were as beautiful as any of the other flowers there.

Names around the world

French	Pâquerette, Petite Marguerite
German	Gänseblümchen
Spanish	Margarita común
Welsh	Llygad y dydd
Polish	Stokrotka pospolita, stokrotka łąkowa, stokrotka trwała
Swedish	Tusenskōna

Your name for this plant

....

How can I recognize Daisies and where can I find them?

Probably one of the easiest plants to find and recognize, the Daisy grows in grassy areas, such as playing fields, lawns and verges. It is a small flower, with a bright yellow centre surrounded by a halo of long, narrow, white petals.

All parts of the Daisy are edible but you might find the leaves a little bitter. The flowers tend to taste better on a hot day, since the sunshine warms up the pollen.

Daisy Bruise Salve

We're more likely to get bruised during the summer months when we spend more time outdoors – luckily, that's when Daisies are in plentiful supply! Rub this salve on your skin any time you get a bump or a knock, and see how much better your skin feels afterwards.

Makes 125g (4½oz)

enough daisy flower heads to fill the jar (make sure the flowers are clean, but don't wash them)
sunflower or vegetable oil, to cover
beeswax (see method for quantity)
a couple of drops of lavender oil (optional)

❶ Place the daisies in an 150-ml (5-fl oz/⅔-cup) jar with a lid, pressing them down a little but not packing them in too tightly. Then pour over enough oil to cover, screw on the lid and leave in a sunny place for 2 weeks.

❷ Strain the daisies through a fine-mesh sieve (strainer) set over a measuring jug, squeezing out as much oil as you can. Measure the amount of oil collected – you will need a quarter the volume of oil in beeswax. So, if you made 100ml (3½fl oz/½ cup) of the oil, you will need 25g (¾oz) beeswax.

❸ Put the oil and beeswax into a bowl, then set the bowl in a larger pan filled with about 3cm (1in) water (make sure that the water does not get into the oil mixture). Place over a low heat and melt the beeswax into the oil, stirring gently with a wooden skewer. Stir in the lavender oil, if using, then take the pan off the heat. Pour a little of the wax mixture on to a cold saucer and wait for a few minutes to see how it sets. It needs to have the consistency of an ointment, so you may need to add a little extra beeswax or oil to get it right.

❹ Once you have the proportions correct, heat the mixture again until it is liquid, then pour into small lidded jars or into an ice-cube tray (you can store it in the freezer for when you need it – just make sure no-one tries to eat it!).

Dandelion
Taraxacum officinale

Habitat: Anywhere and everywhere

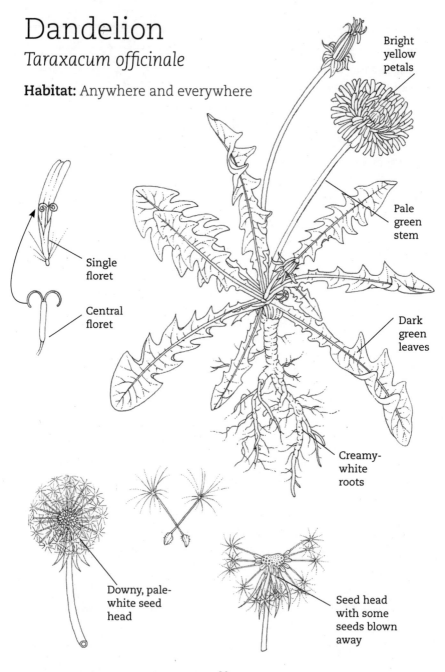

Bright yellow petals

Pale green stem

Dark green leaves

Single floret

Central floret

Creamy-white roots

Downy, pale-white seed head

Seed head with some seeds blown away

How can I recognize Dandelions and where can I find them?

This is one of the best-known plants on the planet. You'll find Dandelions wherever there's a patch of grassy ground with a sunny aspect. You'll see a clump of either irregularly jagged or smooth-edged leaves, which taper elegantly into the ground, radiating out from a central rosette. From early spring onwards, the bright yellow flower, with its many long, slim petals, emerges from the centre of the leaves. The stem can be up to 20cm (8in) tall, and is hollow. In the summer, the snapped stem will ooze a white liquid, which can occasionally irritate skin. Bear this in mind and don't be tempted to nibble at the stem (the rest of the plant is fine).

As the flower ages, the petals are replaced with over 200 seed heads, making a soft, white, downy globe at the top of the stem. If you blow gently on this downy globe, the white seed heads detach and drift away. The number of times you have to blow before all the seedheads have gone is supposed to tell you the time! Generations of

---

Names around the world

French Pisenlit

German Lowenzahn

Spanish Diente de leon

Welsh Dant y llew

Polish Mlecz, Dmuchawiec

Swedish Maskros

Your name for this plant:

....

It's interesting to note that the common name for the Dandelion is the same in all these countries, except one. Most names translate as "tooth of the lion", because of the typical, jagged, tooth-like shape of the leaves. The French name, however, means "wet the bed". Find out why further on!

children have done this – try it: it may or may not be accurate...

More about Dandelions

It's funny how the most common plants (Dandelions included) tend to be the most useful ones.

Despite that, because Dandelions are so prolific, some gardeners wage a war on them, spraying them with weed-killer or digging them up. If you know someone like this, arm yourself with some of the information here and tell them to relax.

Dandelions are so beautiful that, if they weren't free and you could only buy them from garden centres, they'd probably cost quite a lot of money.

Not only that, they're a vitally important food source for bees, grasshoppers, butterflies and, very specifically, the bald-faced hornet.

The petals can be used raw in salads or popped into rice at the end of the cooking time (where they add a delicate floral flavour), or they can be used to make jam. The leaves too can be torn into small pieces and eaten raw in a salad, their bitterness perking up bland lettuce leaves (remember that you don't need many – one medium leaf mixed into a salad is enough for four–six people).

Dandelion roots can be paired with those of Burdock (see p.78) to make a delicious drink – Dandelion and Burdock. Or they can be made into a powder (see p.95), for flavouring drinks or other recipes.

As well as being beautiful, nutritious and good to eat, Dandelions have been used as medicine for hundreds of years – we know this from the inclusion of the word "officinale" in the Latin name, which means "medicinal". The French name for the plant, "pisenlit", means "wet the bed" and refers to its use as a diuretic (this is a medicine that helps you pee if you have problems doing so). Don't worry, though, handling or eating Dandelions will not cause any embarrassment!

Become a Dandelion farmer

It is highly likely that you will become very enthusiastic about Dandelions – quite right too, given what you know about them. I even know of a garden centre whose enterprising owners grow individual Dandies in terracotta pots, which they sell for a surprising amount of money, and why not?

If you grow your own Dandelions, in a sandy soil, you will get long, fat roots that are easy to harvest and cost nothing.

Try growing them in a pot first – you can expand to raised beds when you're an expert!

Find a large plant pot (or a bucket with a hole in the bottom) and pop some bits of broken pottery or rocks in the bottom for drainage. Fill the rest of the bucket with a mix of three-quarters ordinary garden soil and one-quarter sand. Moisten with water, then gather together six or seven Dandelion "clocks" and press them into the soil. Place in a sunny spot. Water occasionally and watch them grow.

Dandelion root powder

You might have seen something called "Dandelion coffee" in health food stores. It's true that Dandelion roots do make a good coffee substitute, but we're going to do something much more

interesting with them here. We're going to use the sweet, caramelly, nutty taste of Dandelion root to flavour chocolate cream truffles.

If you have any experience of growing root vegetables such as carrots, turnips or potatoes, you'll know that they're harvested mainly in the autumn (fall) and winter months. Dandelion roots work in the same way. If you try to harvest them in the summer, you'll find that the ground may well be too hard, baked dry in the heat of the sun, and incredibly difficult to chisel into with even the sharpest of spades. Secondly, even if you do manage to dig up some roots, they're likely to be too small and skinny to be worth the bother.

So, wait for an autumn (fall) or winter's day when the soil is moist and find the biggest clumps of Dandelions, since they will have the biggest roots. Wear old clothes – you're likely to get muddy! Push your spade or trowel into the soil a few inches away from the Dandelion plant (so you don't slice up the roots) and lever the plant out of the soil. You might as well gather quite a few and do them all at once since it is quite messy.

You'll need three or four medium-sized roots to make enough powder for the recipe on p.97. Try to dig up as much of the long tap root as possible. The spindly bits are fine to harvest, too. Remove the leaves.

Next, wash the roots. Break off as much of the clumpy mud as possible, then put the roots in a bucket. Rinse them repeatedly in cold running water – an outside tap is probably best for this job. Some of the larger bits of root will have a "skin", a bit like potato peel. Don't worry about it.

Then, chop the roots, either in a food processor or with a sharp knife. You will need to enlist the help of a tame adult whichever method you use.

Put the chopped roots into a bowl of clean water, agitating them with your hands – the water will go slightly milky. Rinse and repeat until the water runs clear. This will remove any bitterness.

Now dry out the roots. There are two ways:

a) The most energy-efficient way is to spread the roots out on a sheet of paper in a room which has a regular temperature, making sure that the bits are not touching each other (otherwise they can go mouldy). This will take about one week.

b) If you can't wait, set your oven to a very low heat (110°C/225°F/ Gas mark ¼). If you have a range cooker, such as an Aga, use the coolest part. Spread the roots in an even layer on a baking sheet and pop into the oven. It should take about 2 hours to dry the roots thoroughly. They will feel brittle when they're done and will break easily.

Leave the roots to cool completely, then grind them to a fine powder in a spice or coffee grinder. Store in an airtight jar – it will keep indefinitely. You can use the powder in the next recipe (p.97) or as a drink (some people drink it instead of coffee; you make it in a cafetière, just as you would make a pot of ordinary ground coffee).

These scrummy truffles are well worth the time it takes to make them. You will need to let the cream set overnight in the refrigerator.

Dandelion Cream Truffles

Makes 25–30 truffles

100ml (3½fl oz/scant ½ cup) double (heavy) cream

3 tsp dandelion root powder (see p. 95)

400g (14oz/2⅔ cups) white chocolate, broken into small pieces

50g (2oz/3½ tbsp) unsalted butter, chopped into small pieces

2 tsp vanilla extract

300g (10½oz/2 cups) milk or dark (bittersweet) chocolate, broken into small pieces

❶ Put the double (heavy) cream and the dandelion root powder into a pan and gradually bring to the boil. Remove from the heat and add the white chocolate pieces, leaving them to melt into the hot cream. Add the butter and leave to cool even further.

❷ When the mixture is just warm, add the vanilla extract and beat lightly with a metal spoon to mix thoroughly. Transfer the mixture to a container with a lid and pop into the refrigerator for 2 hours to harden.

❸ Scoop out chunks of the mixture and roll into neat balls, about 2cm/¾in in diameter. Put them in a container, with sheets of greaseproof (wax) paper between each layer, and put them in the freezer overnight. The next day, line a baking sheet with greaseproof (wax) paper.

❹ Place the milk or dark chocolate in a heatproof bowl set over a pan of simmering water. Make sure the base of the bowl does not touch the water and be careful not to splash any water into the chocolate, otherwise it won't set. Let the chocolate melt – don't be tempted to stir it.

❺ Using 2 forks, dip each truffle into the chocolate, covering it completely, then place onto the lined baking sheet. It's a good idea to get the baking sheet as close as you can to the chocolate. Leave to set in a cool place (this will take a matter of minutes).

Dandelion, Onion and Red Pepper Frittata

This is an unusual way to use up an excess of Dandelion flowers.

❶ Preheat the oven to 180°C/350°F/Gas Mark 4 or the grill (broiler) to high.

❷ Melt the oil and the butter together in a large, heavy, oven-proof frying pan (skillet) over a medium-low heat. Add the pepper and onion, turn the heat up to medium and sauté for 4–5 minutes, until soft but not soggy. Add the dandelion flowers and stir gently, then put the lid on the pan, turn the heat down to low and cook for 2 minutes.

❸ Meanwhile, in large jug (pitcher), beat the eggs with the milk, then stir in the chopped herbs and some salt and pepper.

❹ Pour the beaten egg mixture into the pan, turn the heat back up to medium and cook until the bottom has set, about 3 minutes. Sprinkle with the grated cheese, then put the pan in the oven or under the grill (broiler), for 3–4 minutes, until the top is set and golden.

Serves 4–6

1 tbsp vegetable oil

50g (1¾oz/3½ tbsp) butter

1 red pepper, thinly sliced

1 large red onion, finely chopped

30–40 fresh dandelion flowers (stems removed, sliced across the bottom of the flower, leaving the frilled green part but removing the bulbous part)

6–8 eggs

1l (35fl oz/4¼ cups) milk

a handful of fresh herbs, coarsely chopped (use whatever you have to hand – this could include garden herbs, as well as Ground Elder, Wintercress, Hairy Bittercress, Jack-by-the-Hedge)

70g (2½oz/1 cup) grated hard cheese, such as Parmesan

salt and freshly ground black pepper, to taste

Fat Hen
Chenopodium album

Habitat: Wasteland, turned soil, anywhere and everywhere

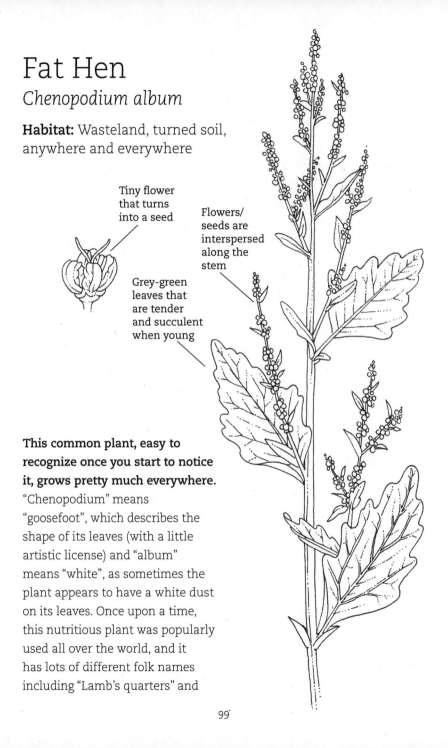

Tiny flower that turns into a seed

Flowers/ seeds are interspersed along the stem

Grey-green leaves that are tender and succulent when young

This common plant, easy to recognize once you start to notice it, grows pretty much everywhere. "Chenopodium" means "goosefoot", which describes the shape of its leaves (with a little artistic license) and "album" means "white", as sometimes the plant appears to have a white dust on its leaves. Once upon a time, this nutritious plant was popularly used all over the world, and it has lots of different folk names including "Lamb's quarters" and

"Pigweed" as well as "Goosefoot". It's still very popular in India, and is also used by some of the top chefs on the planet. It is likely to have been given the name "Fat Hen" since chickens like it and, presumably, at one time it was used for fattening them up!

It is readily available and tasty. Its leaves, just like those of spinach, are rich in calcium, iron and protein. As a wild food, it has a great deal of value so it's easy to imagine why it was once so popular and also, quite frankly, mind-boggling to think that so few people know what it is these days.

If you've heard of quinoa (a grain that looks a little bit like couscous, that has a lovely nutty flavour) then you may be intrigued to know that Fat Hen is actually a close cousin.

You can eat Fat Hen raw in salads or sandwiches, or steamed as a side dish (it's lovely with butter, pepper and a little lemon juice) or even as a part of a pie filling. However, if you'd like to try cooking something a little more interesting with it, I've given you a recipe for a traditional Indian dish (see p.101).

> ## Names around the world
>
> | | |
> |---|---|
> | **French** | Chénopode blanc |
> | **German** | Weißer gänsefuß |
> | **Spanish** | Cenizo |
> | **Welsh** | Troed yr ŵydd |
> | **Polish** | Lebioda |
> | **Swedish** | Srinm ålla |
> | **Hindi** | Bathua |
>
> **Your name for this plant:**
>
> ....

How can I recognize Fat Hen and where can I find it?

This common plant, easy to recognize once you start to notice it, grows pretty much everywhere. Fat Hen can grow up to 2m (6½ft) tall, although it is usually smaller than that, with an average height of 1m (3¼ft). It often has reddish-coloured stems (although not always – sometimes they're green-grey), diamond-shaped green leaves, which are usually toothed (although not always – sometimes they're smooth) and spiked clusters of small white flowers. It sometimes looks as though it is covered in a fine white powder. This is a normal feature of the plant and nothing to worry about.

This is a great way of mixing together a common wild plant with exotic spices. Feel free to adjust the spice to a level that you and the other diners are happy with.

Bathua Curry with Potatoes and Peas

Serves 2 as a main or 4 as a side

2 tbsp vegetable oil

1 large onion, peeled and finely chopped

3-cm (1-in) piece of fresh ginger, peeled and grated

4 garlic cloves, crushed

250g (9oz) potatoes, diced into 2-cm (¾-in) chunks

1 medium-sized fresh red chilli, sliced into thin rings (don't worry about de-seeding it)

2 tsp curry powder

salt to taste

250g (9oz) frozen peas

2 tbsp coconut milk

250–300g (9–10½oz) fresh Fat Hen leaves

❶ Heat the oil in a large frying pan (skillet) over a medium heat. Add the onion, ginger and garlic, and fry, stirring, for 3 minutes. Add the potatoes, sliced chilli, curry powder and a little salt, then continue to cook, stirring gently, for 5 minutes.

❷ Add the frozen peas and coconut milk, turn the heat down a little, cover with a lid, and cook for 10 minutes.

❸ Remove the lid and check to see if the potatoes are nice and soft – a knife should pierce through one easily. Add the fat hen leaves, stir to combine, then cover and cook for a further 5 minutes.

❹ Serve with naan bread for scooping up the tasty sauce.

Greater Plantain
Plantago major

Habitat: Grassland, verges, roadsides... anywhere where people tread

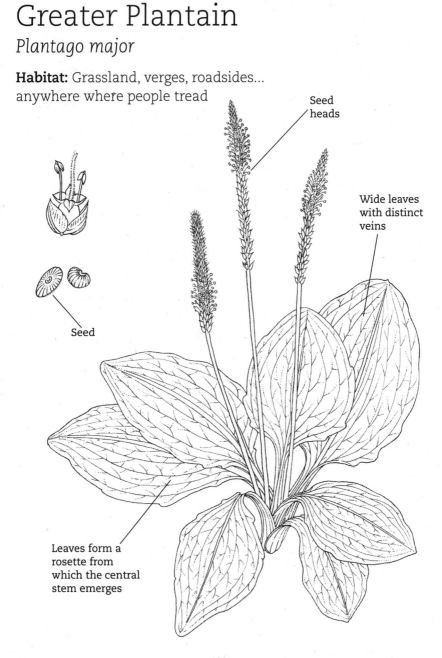

Seed heads

Wide leaves with distinct veins

Seed

Leaves form a rosette from which the central stem emerges

How can I recognize Greater Plantain and where can I find it?

Greater Plantain is identified by its smooth, oval leaves, which radiate out into a rosette, 5–20cm (2–8in) long, and 4–9cm (1½–3½in) wide. These leaves have between five and nine distinct veins, running up the stalk and into the leaf, which become more prominent the older the leaves get. If you nip out the bottom of the stalk you can see the ends of the "threads" of the veins; pull these gently and you will see the leaf pucker up. Later in the season, the flower spike appears, rising from the centre of the rosette. This spike can be up to 20cm (8in) long. The top half of it contains a thick cluster of tiny flowers which turn into seeds. Only a few of the flowers along the seed head will be in bloom at any one time.

Quite a few of the plants in this book are ones that you are likely to walk past every day without noticing.

Greater Plantain (also called Broadleaf Plantain) is a good example of this. It grows anywhere and everywhere; along verges, along paths, in the margins of open grassland, and is also very likely to be found in your garden too. It likes to grow in ground that has been disturbed, especially at the edges of fields or other grassy areas. Its Welsh name, which translates as "the old wide thing of the roadway", comes from a time before we had cars and other motorized transport; the plant was spread along roadways as people picked up its seeds in the soles of their boots and trod them into the ground as they went along their way.

If you bear in mind that each plant can produce up to 20,000 tiny seeds, you can begin to understand why it can be found just about everywhere!

Although it is native to Northern Europe and parts of Asia, Greater Plantain has spread, in the way described above, all over the world. It's for this reason that Native American tribes called it "White Mens' Footsteps". It was also at one time called "Cart Track Plant".

This plant positively thrives from harsh treatment, and loves to colonise disturbed ground anywhere.

What to do with Greater Plantain

Greater Plantain leaves are edible and incredibly nutritious, containing calcium as well as vitamins A, C and K, but (tragically) they are not the most delicious (or easy) plant to eat. The young leaves, soft and tender, are OK and can be included with other young leaves in a salad, but the older leaves are extremely tough and need to be cooked. Arguably, this is a survival food rather than something which would be eaten for pleasure. However, there are a couple of quirky things that this plant does that you need to know about.

Here's something for you to try out:

A: The Smell Test

Greater Plantain leaves can add a very distinctive fragrance to cooking. I'm not going to tell you what that fragrance is... See if you can guess by following the instructions below!

❶ On a dry day, find 3 or 4 Greater Plantain leaves that are not too muddy.

❷ Scrumple them up in your hands.

❸ Start to rub the leaves between your hands, first slowly, then faster, as you get used to the sensation. Rub them vigorously together for at least 2 minutes. The reason you're doing this is to heat up the plant so that it releases its oils – it's these oils which produce the scent and the flavour.

4 Stop rubbing and sniff the pulpy leaves. Are they giving off an aroma that is familiar?

Not everyone is able to give a name to a scent without any clues, so I'll tell you that the slightly soggy leaves in your hands smell like mushrooms and/or truffle oil (truffle oil is very rare and expensive and is often used in Italian cooking). Lots of people like the flavour of mushrooms, but not the texture, so a good way to use Greater Plantain leaves in cooking is to use them to create mushroomy flavours. Make a risotto (I've given you a recipe for this on p.106).

B: The Moisturizer

For now, drop those leaves and see what your hands feel like. They'll be damp at first but, as they dry, you will find that the juice from the leaves will make your hands feel super soft.

C: The Healer

Although I haven't included a lot of medicinal uses for plants in this book, Greater Plantain is exceptionally effective at (and was once in common use for) treating stings, bites, cuts, scrapes and bleeding. The leaves are both anti-inflammatory and antibacterial. To use, simply squish up the leaves (see above) to release the juices, and apply to the wound for as long as necessary.

Risotto with Greater Plantain Leaf "Truffle" Oil

Mimic the taste of truffle in this risotto by using nutritious plantain leaves in its stead for a hint of luxury on the cheap!

Serves 4–6

1½ teaspoons vegetable oil

generous knob of butter

1 red onion, finely chopped

2 garlic cloves, crushed

300g (10½oz/1½ cups) risotto rice (preferably Arborio)

900ml (32fl oz/scant 4 cups) vegetable stock

70g (2½oz/generous ½ cup) frozen peas

200g (7oz) strong Cheddar cheese, finely grated

8 large greater plantain leaves, washed and patted dry

green salad, to serve

❶ Melt the oil and butter in a large frying pan (skillet), preferably with a lid, over a medium heat. Add the onion and cook, stirring, for about 7 minutes, then add the garlic and cook for a further minute, until golden.

❷ Turn the heat down a little and add the rice, stirring continually for a minute or so, until the grains are covered in the oil/butter. Don't let the rice burn!

❸ Add half the stock, then turn the heat to medium and cook for 10 minutes, stirring all the time.

❹ Adding the remaining stock, little by little, stirring well so that the rice absorbs the liquid gradually. Add the peas, lower the heat again, put the lid on the pan, and cook for a further 15 minutes, stirring occasionally, until all the liquid has been absorbed.

❺ Stir in the cheese, then remove the pan from the heat. Pop the greater plantain leaves on top of the rice, put the lid on the pan (or cover it with foil) and let it stand for 10 minutes before serving, so that the flavour of the leaves can infuse the rice.

❻ Remove the plantain leaves and give the risotto a final stir before serving, with a salad on the side.

Ground Elder
Aegopodium podagraria

Habitat: Wasteland near gardens, verges, hedgerows, lanes and tracks

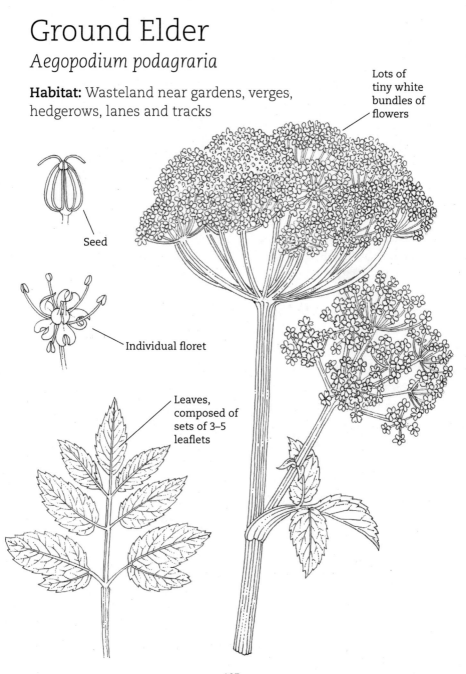

Lots of tiny white bundles of flowers

Seed

Individual floret

Leaves, composed of sets of 3–5 leaflets

How can I recognize Ground Elder and where can I find it?

Ground Elder grows prolifically – you can find it on wasteland, in hedgerows, in parks (often tucked away on the fringes of the grassy areas) and in gardens, where it's very common for gardeners to be completely at a loss as to how to get rid of the stuff.

Left to its own devices, this innocent-looking plant will take over the entire garden, leaving no space for anything else to grow!

If it is a mild winter, you can find Ground Elder throughout the year. The plant is so-named because the leaves look very similar to those of the Elder tree (see p.54). The young, fresh leaves are folded up, soft to the touch and shiny. As the leaves get older they open, revealing three groups of three leaves, with finely toothed edges and a matte finish. Later in the year, flat-topped clusters of tiny white flowers appear on stems that can be up to 60cm (24in) in height. These upside-down-umbrella-shaped bundles of tiny flowers are sometimes called "umbels".

Archaeological evidence has shown that the Romans deliberately carried Ground Elder with them, which certainly would have helped the plant spread around the world, so they must have had good reason to bring it along.

It's a very tasty and nutritious vegetable, but Ground Elder has additional qualities, which are explained by its folk names.

Names around the world

French	Egopode
German	Gewöhnlicher giersch/ Geißfuß
Spanish	Egopodio o hierba de san andres
Welsh	Onnen y ddaear (ground ash) or Cythraul y gerddi (devil of the gardens)
Polish	Podagrycznik pospolity
Swedish	Kirskål

Your name for this plant:

....

There are least two folk names for this plant: one of these is Gout Weed, the other is Bishops' Weed. This is because the plant is a very good treatment for gout, a type of arthritis which is sometimes (but not always) made worse by eating very rich food and drinking red wine. Once upon a time, bishops would have commonly suffered from gout since they were given the very best wines and meats, because of their high status in the church. This plant can certainly help ease the pain of this illness.

Serving suggestion

The young, folded-up leaves are the tastiest ones to eat raw. They make a great addition to a salad, since they have a peppery, celery-like flavour, with a little bit of lemon thrown in. The older leaves are still very good to eat, but benefit from steaming (just 30 seconds should be enough). Eat them with a little oil or butter, and salt and pepper, as a nutritious side dish to a main meal. They also work well wilted on top of a pizza!

If you know any keen gardeners (who will very likely have Ground Elder, which they are unable to get rid of, growing in their gardens), tell them about the plant's edible properties. Perhaps you can persuade them that, instead of a patch of annoying weeds, they actually have a crop of tasty greens!

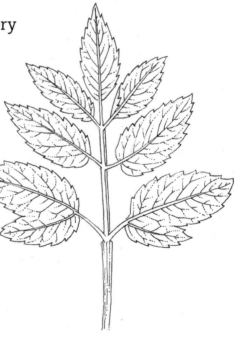

Ground Ivy
Glechoma hederacea

Habitat: Shady places, long grass, edges and verges

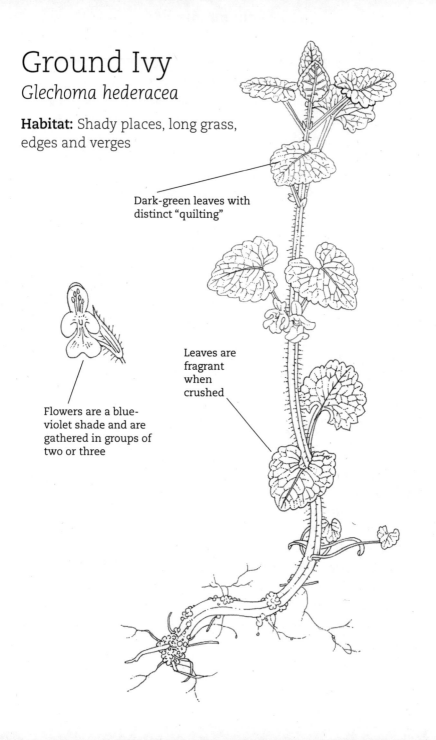

Dark-green leaves with distinct "quilting"

Flowers are a blue-violet shade and are gathered in groups of two or three

Leaves are fragrant when crushed

Ground Ivy is a member of the mint family and, despite the name, actually nothing to do with ivy (which is not edible, by the way).

The name is due to its sprawling, rambling way of growing. Although the plant originated in Europe, at one time it was highly regarded all over the world.

Ground Ivy has both culinary and medicinal uses: it can be used in salads, where its aromatic, flavoursome leaves add a peppery sort of flavour; it can be steeped to make a herbal tea; it was also used, at one time, as rennet (to make cheese set). There are numerous claims for the plant's use as a cough medicine, but this has not yet been scientifically proven.

We do get a clue to one of its major uses, though, by its folk names: "Alehoof" in particular. "Ale" because it was used in brewing, not only to add flavour but to clarify and preserve beer. The "hoof" part of the folk name is because people believed that the leaf looked a bit like a hoof. Other names include "Creeping Charlie", "Blue Runner" (because of the little blue flowers), "Hay Maids", "Catsfoot" and "Run-Away-Robin".

Several butterflies, including the Orange Tip and the Marsh Fritillary, rely on Ground Ivy as a source of nectar. The Red Twin-Spot Carpet Moth also uses it for food.

How can I recognize Ground Ivy and where can I find it?
This plant has circular, fan-shaped leaves, up to 3cm (1in) in diameter, which are a little hairy on top. These leaves are carried on stems up to 6cm (2½in) long. The stems

---

Names around the world

French Lierre terrestre
German Gewöhnlicher gundermann
Spanish Hiedra
Welsh Eiddew'r ddaear (literal) or mantell Fair
Polish Bluszczyk ziemny
Swedish Jordreva

Your name for this plant:

....

have a square profile (nip off the stem and look down the length from where you've cut and you'll see what I mean).

When in blossom in the spring, Ground Ivy has small, tubular-shaped, blue-violet flowers, gathered in clumps of two or three. In spring and summer, these little blobs of colour are visible in long grass, giving away the presence of the plant.

When crushed, Ground Ivy gives off an unusual, slightly medicinal scent, which is very pungent. Like many small plants, ground ivy is often overlooked, hidden underneath bolder, bushier plants or in long grasses. It will grow in forested, damp shady areas as well as in full sun.

It can cover large areas: some gardeners regard it as invasive, whilst others grow it in pots.

This just goes to show how people can have different opinions about plants – one person's beauty is another person's weed!

The first time I discovered Ground Ivy, I'd pitched my tent on a large patch of the stuff, and it was the overwhelming scent given off by the crushed leaves which attracted my attention. They're incredibly aromatic, having a scent that people tend to either love or hate.

Heather
Calluna vulgaris

Habitat: Heathland, hilly areas, acid soil

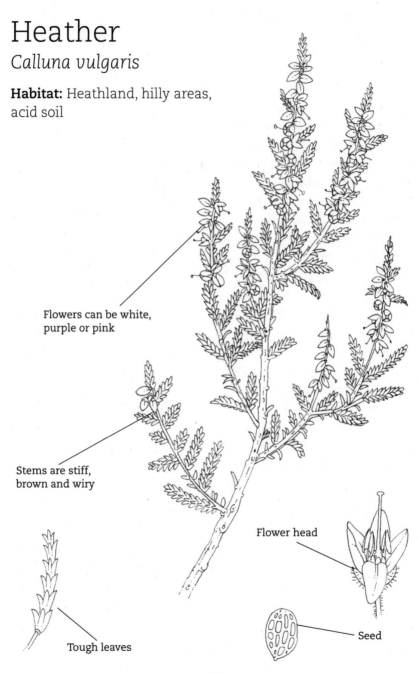

Flowers can be white, purple or pink

Stems are stiff, brown and wiry

Tough leaves

Flower head

Seed

Historically, Heather branches have had many uses: as thatching for houses; as stuffing for mattresses; as firewood; and to make baskets and brooms (the typical brooms that witches fly about on are likely to have been made of Heather); it will also dye wool a yellow colour. In fact, the "Calluna" part of the name is from a Greek word meaning "to sweep clean" or "to make beautiful".

Bees, too, love Heather, and the honey made from these flowers is said to be amongst the best in the world. In the summer months, professional beekeepers will transport their hives to where the heather is, so that their bees can have a good feed!

Heather not only makes a lovely addition to a bath (see p.115), it also makes a refreshing tea (see p.116). Perhaps you could sip a cup of Heather tea whilst lying in a Heather bath?

How can I recognize Heather and where can I find it?

The Heather we're talking about here is also known as Ling Heather or Scotch Heather. It is a low-growing shrubby plant, up to 50cm

Names around the world	
French	Bruyère
German	Besenheide, Heidekraut
Spanish	Flor de brezo
Welsh	Grug mêl
Polish	Wrzos zwyczajny, wrzos pospolity
Swedish	Ljung

Your name for this plant:

....

(1½ft) tall, with brownish, wiry stems and tough, tiny leaves up to 3mm (1/8in) long. During the summer and autumn months the flowers appear – the pinky-purple patches on distant hills are a good way to recognize the plant. Close up, these flowers look like tiny bells. Though small, Heather flowers are abundant, and provide a valuable food source for insects.

Although Heathers are often used in garden planting, in the wild they like open heathland with acidic soil, often in places of some altitude. Bilberries (see p.33) and Heather often grow side-by-side; both plants don't mind poor soil with little nutritional value.

Do you know anyone whose favourite luxury is to have a long soak in a deep bath whilst reading a book? This bath mix will make the experience even better – just be sure that the Heather is well-wrapped in the muslin (cheesecloth) square, otherwise there will be lots of annoying twiggy bits floating in the water!

When you gather your Heather be careful not to pull the plants up by the roots.

For one bath

a few handfuls of heather flowers and stems

20 x 20cm (8 x 8in) piece of muslin (cheesecloth)

ribbon or string

Relaxing Heather Bath Mix

❶ Remove any debris from the heather flowers and stems, then chop up finely.

❷ Top 1 tablespoon of the chopped heather into the middle of the fabric square, then securely tie it up into a bag using the ribbon/string, so that none of the little bits can escape.

❸ Make a loop in the ribbon/string so that you can hang the bag under the running hot water, letting the heather infuse the water with its lovely scent as the bath runs.

Heather Tea

Gather a handful of fresh Heather flowers, stems and leaves on a sunny day and make this simple tea.

For one pot of tea

1 tsp fresh heather (flowers, stems and leaves) per person

boiling water

sugar or honey, to taste

❶ Pick out any debris (such as bits of twig) from your heather. Pop 1 teaspoon per person into a teapot and top with boiling water.

❷ Leave to steep for 5 minutes, then pour into cups through a tea strainer. Add sugar or honey (heather honey would be appropriate!), to taste.

Horseradish
Armoracia rusticana

Habitat: Sunny verges, wasteland, field margins, gardens

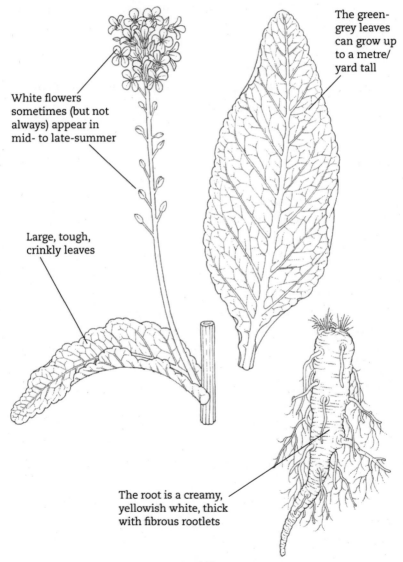

The green-grey leaves can grow up to a metre/yard tall

White flowers sometimes (but not always) appear in mid- to late-summer

Large, tough, crinkly leaves

The root is a creamy, yellowish white, thick with fibrous rootlets

Horseradish originated in western Asia and south-eastern Europe, but now grows just about everywhere. You might imagine that the "horse" part of the name is because horses like eating it, but this is not the case. The name comes from a word meaning "strong" or "coarse" and can apply equally aptly to the tough leaves, the strong smell, and the harsh scent and flavour.

Names around the world

French   Raifort

German   Meerrettich

Spanish   Rábano picante

Welsh   Rhuddygl Poeth (hot radish)

Polish   Chrzan pospolity

Swedish   Pepparrot

Your name for this plant:

....

Wasabi, a Japanese condiment that tastes very similar to Horseradish, belongs to the same plant family, as do cabbages and mustard. Sometimes Horseradish is sold as Wasabi since the two plants are hard to tell apart, taste-wise.

Horseradish is a flavour you may initially hate, but keep trying it. I think it is absolutely delicious – your tastebuds do a crazy dance around your mouth and make you jump up and down on the spot!

It is the roots of Horseradish that are used to make a sauce, which is traditionally served with beef (see the recipe on p.120). Make sure that you have asked permission from the landowner before digging up the root and don't try to pull it up by the leaves – that won't work! It is easiest to dig up when the soil is wet, after rain. Push a spade into the ground about 20cm (8in) from the plant and dig a trench all the way round it. Then, use a trowel to dig around the root, which you will find goes deeply into the ground. Don't worry if you don't manage to get all of the root.

How can I recognize Horseradish and where can I find it?

This plant can easily be mistaken for Common Dock (the plant traditionally used to treat nettle stings). However, once you know what to look for, the differences between Horseradish and Dock become obvious. Horseradish has large, tough, shiny, green/grey leaves, with faintly serrated edges, which will grow up to 1m (3ft) tall; these leaves are distinctly wavy. The whole plant is often seen growing in large clumps. There's something quite understated, yet also showy because of the mass of tall, wavy-edged leaves, about a stand of Horseradish! Dock leaves tend to be smaller, without the waviness or serrations, and don't "clump" in the same way, either.

Horseradish spreads quickly, and you may well see huge masses of it growing on roadsides, riverbanks and waste ground.

If in doubt, simply tear off some of the leaf and crush it in your fingers – a Horseradish plant will give off a pungent scent: peppery, mustardy, sharp and hot. Occasionally, you might see a Horseradish with white flowers, which sometimes (but not always) appear in mid- to late-summer.

Traditional Horseradish Sauce

Horseradish sauce has been made since at least the 16th century. This recipe is very old – apart from the convenient use of a blender! Although it is usually served with roast beef, if you like it try adding it to mashed potato, or as part of a salad dressing with oil and vinegar.

Makes 70g (2½oz)

25-cm (10-in) piece of horseradish root, leaves removed, washed
pinch of salt
pinch of sugar
1 tbsp white wine vinegar

❶ Using a potato peeler, peel the brown skin from the outside of the horseradish root. You will now have a lovely white piece of horseradish.

❷ If possible, do the next part of the recipe outdoors. If this isn't practical, then make sure you are in a well-ventilated space by opening all the windows and doors. Horseradish, when chopped, is incredibly potent.

❸ Chop the root into rough chunks, then put into a food processor with the salt, sugar and 1 tablespoon water. Blend until very fine and smooth. You might need to add a little more water to bring it together. If you find that you've put in too much, then either strain the sauce through a fine-mesh sieve (strainer), or add more grated horseradish. Add the vinegar and give the mixture one more quick blitz.

❹ Carefully spoon the sauce into a sterilized, wide-necked jar (see p.222). It will keep in the refrigerator for up to 1 month.

WARNING: Horseradish has a strong scent and taste. It's a good idea to make the sauce outside so the fumes don't affect you, and to wear goggles to protect your eyes. Wear rubber gloves as an added precaution, just in case your hands have a reaction. An old Russian trick is to freeze the root overnight before cutting into it, to tame the fumes.

Wild Marjoram
Origanum vulgare

Habitat: Verges, areas of poor soils, places with a sunny aspect

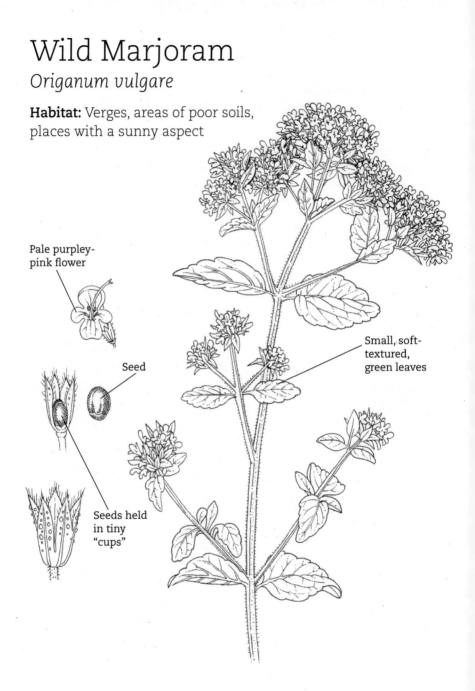

Pale purpley-pink flower

Seed

Seeds held in tiny "cups"

Small, soft-textured, green leaves

Wild Marjoram also goes by the name of Oregano, although there are also cultivated kinds of both plants (they are the same species and often hybridize). They are pretty much interchangeable in recipes, although Wild Marjoram has a stronger flavour than cultivated Marjoram. Wild Marjoram (Oregano) is a very useful kitchen herb, its flavour lending itself well to soups and sauces. My favourite thing to do with it is to sprinkle it on top of a homemade pizza or include it in a loaf of bread! (See p.123.)

How can I recognize Wild Marjoram and where can I find it?

Wild Marjoram is more common than many people realize. It has a strong, thin stem that will grow up to 80cm (2½ft) tall, with small oval leaves carried on short stems. In the late spring and early summer and into the autumn (fall), the plant is distinguishable by its many small pale flowers, which range from white through to purple in colour.

Names around the world

French Origan
German Oregano
Spanish Orégano
Welsh Oregano
Polish Lebiodka pospolita
Swedish · Kungsmynta

Your name for this plant:

....

Although Wild Marjoram prefers chalky or limestone soils, it will happily thrive just about anywhere, with the exception of very soggy ground. Hedgerows, garden borders, verges and wasteland can all accommodate this plant.

The best way to identify Wild Marjoram is by its scent, which is refreshing, spicy and a little peppery.

Try a warm slice of this bread straight from the oven, topped with butter and strong cheese. Delicious!

Wild Marjoram and Onion Bread

Makes 1 loaf

500g (18oz/3⅔ cups) strong white bread flour, plus extra for dusting
2 tsp salt
7g (¼oz) sachet of fast-action (instant active dried) yeast
1 tbsp finely chopped fresh wild marjoram leaves and flowers (or 1½ tsp dried marjoram or oregano)
1 medium onion, finely diced
3 tbsp olive oil, plus extra for oiling
275ml (10fl oz/1¼ cups) warm water

❶ Put the flour, salt, yeast and wild marjoram into a large bowl and stir to combine. Make a dip in the middle of the mixture, add the onion, pour in the oil and water and mix to form a dough.

❷ Dust your work surface with flour and turn the dough out onto it. Knead for 10 minutes, until smooth and springy. Oil a large bowl and put the dough into it, cover with a clean dish towel and leave in a warm place to rise until doubled in size (this could take up to 2 hours, depending on the warmth of the room).

❸ Sprinkle a little more flour over the work surface and turn the dough out onto it. Knock back the dough (this means give it a punch), shape into a ball and place on an oiled baking sheet. Cover with a clean dish towel and leave in a warm place to rise again, until doubled in size. This will take about 1 hour.

❹ Meanwhile, preheat the oven to 220°C/425°F/Gas Mark 7.

❺ Use a sharp knife to cut a cross in the top and dust more flour over the top of the dough. Bake on the middle shelf of the hot oven for 30–40 minutes, until golden on the top. To check whether the loaf is baked, turn it upside down and tap it on the bottom – it should sound hollow. If not, pop it back in the oven for another 10 minutes, then try again. Leave to cool on a wire cooling rack. Be patient – eating half-baked dough can give you a tummy ache.

Wild Mints
Mentha arvensis & Mentha aquatica

Two Wild Mints

The Mint family is a large one – the botanical name for this group of plants is "Lamiaceae" and includes Dead Nettles (which look very much like Nettles, but don't sting), Ground Ivy, Marjoram, Thyme, and many others. There are at least 15 different species of Mint, some of which might have escaped from gardens and naturalized in the wild. Mints easily hybridize with one another (to "hybridize" means to "mix"), so some of the wild ones are impossible to name. Here, I've chosen two types of Mint that you are most likely to find.

All Mints, and all parts of the plant, are edible. They all smell "minty" (although with different scents). If you cut the stem of any Mint, you'll see that it has a square profile.

Mints have been used for thousands of years, all over the planet, for similar reasons, particularly to help with digesting food. It is for this reason that we still eat after-dinner mints today.

Mint was also used to keep insects away in the days before carpets. Mint leaves were strewn on the floor – when they were crushed underfoot, the scent of the leaves deterred insects.

Corn Mint
Mentha arvensis

Habitat: Damp places

How can I recognize Corn Mint and where can I find it?

Corn Mint, as you'd imagine, grows at the edges of fields, but also in the damp shade of hedgerows, in wooded clearings and on wasteland. It reaches a height of about 60cm (24in). As opposed to the Water Mint, it does not grow submerged in water and its leaves are smaller and narrower, paler-coloured and matte, rather than glossy and dark. Its flowers grow in little bundles, at regular intervals along the stem, and are a pale lilac colour.

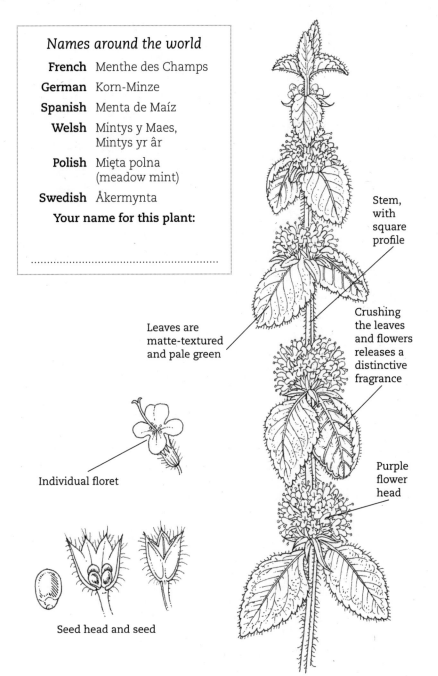

Names around the world

French Menthe des Champs

German Korn-Minze

Spanish Menta de Maíz

Welsh Mintys y Maes, Mintys yr âr

Polish Mięta polna (meadow mint)

Swedish Åkermynta

Your name for this plant:

....

Stem, with square profile

Leaves are matte-textured and pale green

Crushing the leaves and flowers releases a distinctive fragrance

Individual floret

Purple flower head

Seed head and seed

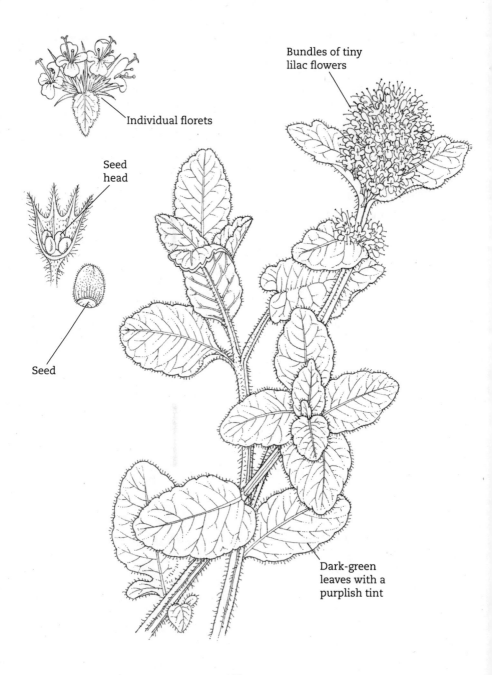

Individual florets

Bundles of tiny
lilac flowers

Seed
head

Seed

Dark-green
leaves with a
purplish tint

Water Mint
Mentha aquatica

Habitat: Damp places

This is one of the commonest Mints. The scent and flavour is interesting, rather like perfume.

How can I recognize Water Mint and where can I find it?

As you'd imagine from the name, Water Mint likes damp places and can often be seen actually growing in water; some of the leaves raised above the level of the water at the edges of streams, rivers or ponds. It can grow to a height of 60cm (24in), and has smooth, oval leaves about 4cm (1½in) long, with blunt serrations along the edges. Water Mint has a distinct purplish tinge to the green leaves and a strong, spicy scent and flavour. The flowers are lilac – bundles of them make a round pom-pom shape at the top of the stem.

Serving suggestions

Mint has a cooling effect, which is why in Morocco Mint tea is given to visitors and guests in little glasses with colourful, gilded decorations. There's no reason to buy Mint tea from stores though, any Wild Mint can be used to make it. Simply pop a sprig of Mint leaves into a cup and top with hot water, adding sugar to taste. Or try adding a sprig to hot chocolate, steep for 5 minutes, then remove before drinking – it's scrummy.

Mint can be torn up and used in salads, added to coleslaw, and used to flavour peas or potatoes. One of my favourite ways of using it is to make Mint Sauce (see p.128).

Homemade Mint Sauce

The perfumed fragrance of Water Mint is a little too overpowering for this recipe, but Corn Mint works very well. You could also use Garden Mint, or a combination of both. Use as a relish for meat or cheese, or stir into a bowl of mushy peas. This might sound strange, but a little Mint Sauce added to a peanut-butter sandwich tastes unusual, but delicious.

Serves 4–6 as a relish

3 handfuls of fresh mint leaves, washed and patted dry

1 tbsp caster (superfine) sugar, or more to taste

60ml (2fl oz/¼ cup) white wine vinegar

a pinch of salt

❶ Chop the mint leaves as finely as you can (a knife, pair of scissors or small blender would all work for this).

❷ Put into a bowl and sprinkle over the sugar.

❸ Put the vinegar in a small saucepan and heat gently until warm, but still easy to touch.

❹ Pour the vinegar over the mint and sugar, then leave to completely cool. Add the salt, have a taste, add more sugar if you think it needs it, then serve.

You can use any kind of Mint you like for this recipe, or a mixture of different kinds. A good rule for Mint is, if you like the scent, you will like the flavour too.

Fresh Mint and White Choc-Chip Ice Cream

Serves 6

400ml (14fl oz/1⅔ cups) whole milk
300ml (10½fl oz/1¼ cups) double
   (heavy) cream
5 drops of vanilla extract
75g (2½oz) fresh mint sprigs, plus extra
   to decorate
4 large egg yolks
140g (5oz/scant ¾ cup) caster
   (superfine) sugar
140g (5oz) white chocolate, frozen then
   smashed into little pieces

❶ Pour the milk and cream into a heavy saucepan with the vanilla extract. Heat gently, stirring, until almost boiling. Remove from the heat, add the mint, then cover and leave for 20 minutes.

❷ Meanwhile, whisk the egg yolks and sugar together in a bowl until thick and pale.

❸ Strain the milk through a sieve (strainer) into a bowl, pressing the mint leaves to release the flavour. Return the infused milk to the pan and bring back to almost boiling point.

❹ Carefully pour half of the hot milk mixture into the egg and sugar mixture and whisk to combine. Then add the rest of the liquid. Return the mixture to the pan and simmer gently, stirring, for 4 minutes, until thickened.

❺ Strain the custard through a fine-mesh sieve (strainer) into a bowl and leave to cool, stirring from time to time to prevent a skin forming on the custard. Cover, and chill overnight.

❻ If you have an ice-cream maker, churn until frozen, adding the chocolate pieces right at the end. If you don't have an ice-cream maker, put the custard into a freezer-proof container with a lid, freeze for 1 hour, then mash well with a fork and stir through the chocolate. Return to the freezer until almost solid.

❼ Serve in glasses with a little sprig of mint to decorate.

Nettles
Urtica dioica

Habitat: Anywhere and everywhere

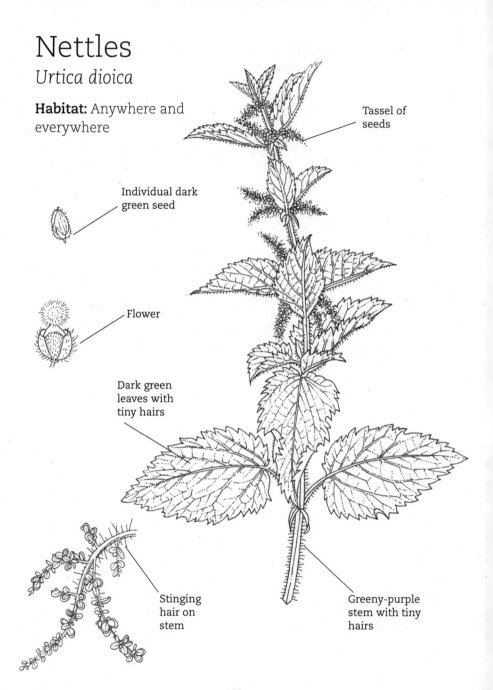

Tassel of seeds

Individual dark green seed

Flower

Dark green leaves with tiny hairs

Stinging hair on stem

Greeny-purple stem with tiny hairs

The "dioica" part of the Nettle's Latin name means "two houses" – this is because the male and female flowers are carried on separate plants. "Urtica" means "to burn" – that part is obvious! The word "nettle" is likely to be derived from an Anglo-Saxon word: "noedl", meaning "needle".

Names around the world

French Ortie
German Nessel
Spanish Ortigas
Welsh Danadl
Polish Pokrzywa zwyczajna
Swedish Nässla
Your name for this plant:

....

How can I recognize Nettles and where can I find them?

Nettles, in one form or another, can be found pretty much everywhere on the planet, without exception. Nettles will grow to up to 2m (6½ft) tall, dying down in the colder months in some places but often visible all year round. The dark green leaves are larger at the bottom of the plant and smaller at the top, varying between 2–15cm (¾–6in) in length. The leaves have small serrations along them, like a saw. The seeds, which appear in the late summer and early autumn (fall), look like long tassels. If you ever pull up the roots of Nettles, you'll see that they are a bright yellow colour.

You might even recognize them by their sting!

More about Nettles

There has always been a particularly close relationship between human beings and Nettles. If you've ever stumbled upon an old, tumbledown, abandoned house, chances are you'd have noticed a stand of Nettles close by. This is because human waste (meaning pee and poo, rather than stuff like broken bottles) adds phosphates and nitrogen to the soil, enriching it and creating the perfect conditions for Nettles to thrive. Although the house may have crumbled and its inhabitants long gone, the Nettles provide us with clues about how people once lived. Lots of plants are examples of a kind of living archaeology.

Nettles are one of the very first plants to colonize places of human habitation, and this might be one of the reasons that some people believe that the Romans introduced Nettles to Britain when they first visited the country some 2000 years ago. As the centurions moved along, exploring, Nettles grew where they'd passed. Actually, Nettles were in Britain already, but the Romans did travel with Nettle seeds for several reasons. Why?

Nettles are edible. We've been eating them for thousands of years. Foragers love Nettles because they're common, they're good for you, and they're very tasty. (In fact, they're sort of like a secret that everyone vaguely knows about.) Not so very long ago, they were called "Poor Man's Spinach".

Nettles make very strong, long-lasting fibre and rope. Humans have been making cloth from Nettles for millennia; some scraps of Nettle cloth, dating back 3,000 years, have been found in Denmark.

Nettles are a medicine. There's a list of folk remedies using them that's as long as your arm, covering just about everything from curing dog bites to an antidote for poison. Folk remedies don't always work, since they're usually based on superstition rather than scientific fact.

Nowadays we can find out what plants are made up of: we know that Nettles are full of iron and vitamin C. You might also be surprised to find that 22% of a Nettle is protein!

The most distinctive feature of the Nettle is its sting. If you have ever been stung by a Nettle, you'll know that it can cause a burning sensation. Both the Romans and some Native American peoples used this to their advantage and used the Nettles to keep themselves warm, by deliberately stinging themselves with bundles of them! This strange habit, admittedly not heard of very much nowadays, is called urtication.

Why do Nettles sting?

Let's be honest, we're not entirely certain why Nettles sting. It has been suggested that they do it to stop animals eating them, but this doesn't explain why all plants don't do the same thing. Thank goodness they don't – salads would be a nightmare! As it happens, not all members of the Nettle family sting. Some of the non-stinging kind are called "Dead Nettles" and they are also good to eat.

How is it that sometimes Nettles sting you, and sometimes they don't?

If you look at a Nettle under a microscope, you'll see that tiny hairs cover the surface of the leaves and stems. Inside each of the hairs is a combination of chemicals, including formic acid and histamines, which sting. If you brush the Nettle, the fragile tips snap off and the hairs injects their "juice" into your skin. If, however, you deliberately take hold of the Nettle, you squash the little hairs flat and reduce the chance of the burn; hence the saying "grasp the nettle", meaning to tackle a problem head-on.

Tiny hairs cover the stems and leaves of Nettles

Do Dock leaves cure Nettle stings?

They help. It's also useful that they always seem to grow close to where the Nettles are. This is because Dock plants are extremely vigorous and will grow just about anywhere. Smaller plants tend to get "drowned out" by Nettles. To find out about a plant that is a hundred times better than Docks for removing stings, see the chapter about Greater Plantain (p.102).

Can you eat raw Nettles?

Yes, you can, although you'd do so mainly as a sort of party trick. Here's how to do it. (You might want to practise first, without an audience.) Bearing in mind the section about how Nettles sting, above, boldly pluck a young Nettle leaf from near the top of the plant.

The paler-coloured leaves are the best. Nip off any remnant of stalk, which tends to be tough.

Fold up the leaf, squashing it as you go to make it more tender.

Eat the leaf, remembering to chew well before you swallow. Make sure you have a bottle of water in case the leaf is fibrous.

You'll find that the raw Nettle leaf has an unexpectedly pleasant taste. I'm not going to tell you what it tastes like, because this might spoil the surprise. Trust me! Now you can astonish your friends.

What is the best time of year to eat Nettles?

In the spring, when fresh new Nettles are coming out of the ground, they are tender, sweet and tasty. Unfortunately, it's at this time that the sting is at its most powerful, so pick with caution and wear a pair of rubber gloves. The top four sets of leaves are the nicest. Nettles grow all year round. Later in the season, Nettles are still fine to eat but will have a stronger, earthier taste, and it's at this time that another edible bit of the Nettle appears: the long, dangling bundles of seed heads.

These are delicious roasted very quickly in a pan, preferably over a camp fire, since all food tastes better outside for some reason.

Cooking with Nettles

We've eaten Nettles for centuries, and continue to do so. We've made them into beer and wine and cordials, and you can buy boxes of Nettle tea in stores. They can be made into soups or used to top poached eggs. In Britain, there's a cheese called Yarg, which is wrapped in dried Nettles.

Oh, by the way... did you know that some brands of gum sweets (such as Haribo™) use Nettles as both a colouring and a flavouring!?

You need to know that removing the stings from Nettles is very easy. Heat will do this for you: either hot water, or heat from the oven. As long as you wear gloves whilst picking and handling, you'll be fine.

Lots of people know that Nettles can be made into a soup, but not so many people have actually eaten it. This recipe is likely to become a firm favourite; as well as being tasty, it's nutritious and costs just pennies to make!

Cream of Nettle Soup with Roasted Garlic

Serves 4

100g (3½oz) (3 good handfuls) fresh
    young nettle leaves
2 large (or 3 small) whole garlic bulbs
3½ tbsp butter
1 tbsp vegetable oil
1 large onion, peeled and chopped
350g (12oz) potatoes, scrubbed, cut into
    evenly sized cubes
600ml (21fl oz/2½ cups) vegetable or
    chicken stock
500ml (17fl oz/2 cups) single (light)
    cream, plus a little extra to serve
salt and freshly ground black pepper

❶ Preheat the oven to 220°C/425°F/Gas Mark 7.

❷ Put the nettle leaves into a colander and rinse thoroughly to remove any dirt. Snip off any bits of stem. Set aside.

❸ Separate the garlic cloves and slice the flat end off of each one. Wrap loosely in a 20-cm (8-in) square of foil and roast in the oven for 20 minutes.

❹ Meanwhile, put the butter and oil into a saucepan set over a medium heat. When the butter is sizzling, add the onion and potato. Cook, stirring, until the onions are golden, about 5 minutes. Add the stock, bring to the simmer, then, cover and cook for 15 minutes.

❺ Remove the garlic from the oven and allow to cool slightly. Squeeze the garlic from its cases into the saucepan, add the nettles and simmer for 10 minutes.

❻ Remove the pan from the heat and let it cool a little. Blend the soup with a hand-held (immersion) blender until smooth, then add the cream, stir well and return to the heat to warm through.

❼ Ladle into soup bowls. Top with a swirl of extra cream and a sprinkle of salt and freshly ground black pepper. Serve with a chunk of lovely fresh bread.

Pineapple Weed
Matricaria discoidea

Habitat: Dry, bare, disturbed ground, such as pathways

Individual flower

Padded flower with a pineapple-like scent

Feathery green leaves and stems

Leaves also have a scent reminiscent of pineapple

How can I recognize Pineapple Weed and where can I find it?

This flower of this plant looks a little like a Daisy that is missing its petals. However, unlike a Daisy, Pineapple Weed can occasionally grow to 20cm (8in) high (although, generally, it grows low – spreading along the ground). The leaves are delicate and feathery.

The best way to identify this plant is by its scent. Rub the bright green, cone-shaped flowerhead between your fingers; you will find that it gives off a lovely fragrance, which smells very much like pineapple (hence the name). Have a nibble on the flower and a bit of the leaf and stalk; as well as smelling like pineapple, this plant tastes of it too. Pineapple Weed also looks a little like another plant, Chamomile, which also has a fragrant scent – a bit like apples. This is why some of its foreign names (see above) refer to it as "Fake Chamomile".

Individual flower head

Names around the world

French Matricaire fausse-camomille, Matricaire sans ligules

German Strahlenlose Kamille

Spanish Manzanilla silvestre

Welsh Camri moch

Polish Rumianek bezpromieniowy

Swedish Gatkamomill

Your name for this plant:

....

If I tell you that this plant likes to travel around on tyres or on the soles of peoples' shoes, I'd be giving you a good hint as to where you might find it.

Pineapple Weed likes to grow in compacted earth, such as you would find at the edges of paths, roads and verges, in dry, gritty soil conditions.

Pineapple-Weed Cordial and Ice Lollies

Makes about 1.5l (52fl oz/6½ cups)

FOR THE CORDIAL:

1.6l (56fl oz/7 cups) water

1.5kg (3lb 6oz/7½ cups) white granulated sugar

zest and juice of 1 lemon

20 Pineapple-Weed flowers, including leaves, washed and patted dry

This recipe was invented by four sisters, aged between six and fifteen, after I took them foraging with a specific purpose in mind. Their grandma had been very ill, and she was looked after by the Macmillan Nurses, who take care of people who are fighting cancer. The girls' grandma recovered and so the girls wanted to raise money to give to the nurses, to help other people with the same illness.

They invented these simple ice lollies and sold them, raising a good sum for the charity, using mainly free ingredients. First, you need to make a simple Pineapple-Weed cordial. You can dilute this with sparkling water and drink it, if you don't fancy making lollipops, or if you can't wait!

❶ Put all the ingredients, except for the pineapple-weed flowers, into a large saucepan and boil until the liquid has reduced by about half. Remove from the heat and, while the liquid is still hot, add the flowers and leave to cool completely.

❷ Once cool, strain to remove the flowers.

❸ Store the cordial in sterilized water bottles (see p.222 for sterilizing instructions). It will keep indefinitely in a refrigerator. You can also freeze it – so be sure to leave 3–4cm (1–1½in) of head-space in the bottles, since water expands when it freezes.

FOR THE LOLLIES:

❶ Simply pour the Pineapple-Weed Cordial into lolly moulds (adding lollipop sticks if necessary) and freeze.

Rosebay Willowherb or Fireweed

Chamerion angustifolium

Habitat: Wasteland, burnt ground, roadsides

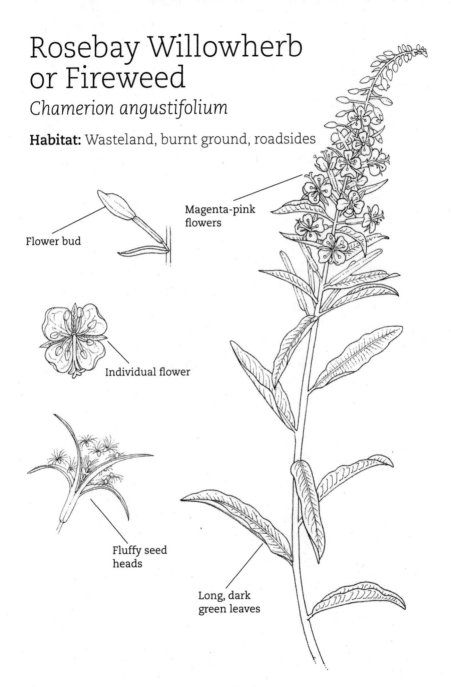

Flower bud

Magenta-pink flowers

Individual flower

Fluffy seed heads

Long, dark green leaves

How can I recognize Rosebay Willowherb and where can I find it?

Easiest to recognize when in flower, this plant grows in large stands, up to 2.5m (8ft) high. The plant has long, narrow leaves ("angustifolium" means "narrow leaved"), which are tapered at both ends and a medium green in colour. In the summer months, the flowers appear – beautiful long spires of magenta pink blossoms, growing towards the top 20cm (8in) of the stems. After the flowers have gone, fluffy white gossamer seed heads form, billowing everywhere in the slightest breeze, demonstrating how easily the plant can spread.

The plant needs sunshine and space to grow. One of the names for this plant is Fireweed, because it thrives in ground that has been burnt. As well as colonizing burnt ground, Rosebay Willowherb will grow on wasteland, roadsides and railway sidings. Sometimes it appears in gardens, but – despite its beauty – most gardeners prefer it in the wild!

In Sweden, Rosebay Willowherb is called Milk Plant, since in the past it was believed that if cattle were fed with it, they would produce more milk.

Serving suggestions

The flowers are edible, sweet, and look pretty in salads. The best parts of this plant, though, are the very young shoots which appear in the spring. Identify your Rosebay Willowherb by noting where it grows in the summer, then return the following year to harvest the young shoots. Wash them thoroughly, then steam them and dress in butter or olive oil, in exactly the way you would serve asparagus.

Names around the world

French	Épilobe à feuilles étroites
German	Weidenröschen
Spanish	Adelfilla
Welsh	Helygwr rhoswellt
Polish	Wierzbówka kiprzyca
Swedish	Mjölkört

Your name for this plant:

....

Sorrel

Rumex acetosa

Habitat: Open grassland, playing fields, heathland

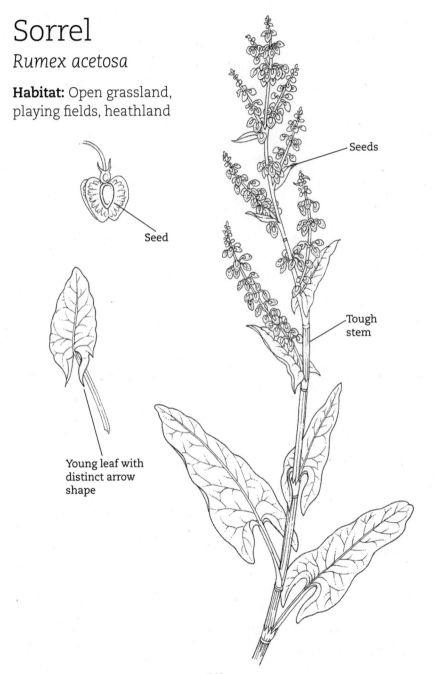

Seed

Seeds

Tough stem

Young leaf with distinct arrow shape

There are a few different kinds of Sorrel, but the one that is most common is described here. There's an edible woodland plant, Wood Sorrel (see p.144), which tastes very similar. Sorrel is also sold as a herb in stores.

The word "Sorrel" comes from an older word meaning "sour". If you like the taste of lemons, then you will really like the taste of this plant. You won't be given much information by the scent, but the flavour is really surprising the first time you try it. The leaf and stem are edible, and people often say that it tastes like the skin of a tart apple. It's also full of vitamin C.

Sorrel is used all over the world. The use of the word "vinegrera" in the Spanish name, matches up with one of the old English names for the plant, "Vinegar Leaf", referring to the tangy flavour. In Eastern Europe, one of the most popular recipes is for a Sorrel soup (see my recipe on p.143).

How can I recognize Sorrel and where can I find it?

Sorrel has smooth leaves that vary in size (depending on the age of the plant) from that of the little fingernail of a child to that of the hand of a large man! The distinguishing feature of Sorrel is that the leaf has a small arrow-shaped nick where it meets the stalk. Also, you'll sometimes see a clump of Sorrel with a single scarlet leaf – keep your eyes peeled when walking in open grassland, especially in places where sheep might have grazed, or open heathland, playing fields and football pitches. As long as it is growing in a place that is not grazed or mown, Sorrel will reach a height of 60cm (24in), producing a tall stem with straggly-looking leaves and tiny red flowers covering the top 10–15cm (4–6in).

Names around the world

French	Oseille Sauvage
German	Sauerampfer
Spanish	Acedera común, Acedera vinegrera
Welsh	Suran
Polish	Szczaw zwyczajny
Swedish	Ängssyra

Your name for this plant:

....

This kind of soup is enjoyed in many parts of Europe, including Russia, Latvia, Germany, Hungary, and Poland, though it is unlikely that you will find it in a supermarket. The egg is traditional, but you can leave it out if you wish.

Sorrel Soup

Serves 4

1 tbsp butter

splash of vegetable oil

2 shallots or onions, peeled and finely chopped

100g (3½oz) sorrel leaves and stems, coarsely chopped, plus extra to garnish

2 tbsp plain (all-purpose) flour

800ml (28fl oz/scant 3½ cups) vegetable stock

125ml (4fl oz/½ cup) single (light) cream

1 egg yolk

salt and freshly ground black pepper, to taste

crusty bread and butter, to serve

❶ Melt the butter and oil in a heavy saucepan over a low heat. Add the shallot or onion and fry gently for about 5 minutes, until golden and translucent. Add the sorrel leaves and stems, and cook until wilted and soft – this will only take a few minutes. Remove the pan from the heat and sift in the flour, then return to the heat and stir briskly with a wooden spoon until the flour has turned a pale brown colour.

❷ Add the stock a little at a time, whisking between each addition so that the mixture doesn't become lumpy. Put the lid on the pan, and simmer for 15 minutes.

❸ Remove from the heat and leave to cool for a few minutes. Then, use a hand-held (immersion) blender to blend the soup to a smooth consistency.

❹ In another bowl, whisk together the cream and the egg yolk, then gently stir into the soup.

❺ Season with salt and pepper and serve garnished with a couple of extra sorrel leaves, added just before serving so they don't wilt too much. Make sure you have a nice loaf of crusty bread, sliced and buttered, to go with it.

Wood Sorrel

Oxalis acetosella

Habitat: Long-established deciduous woodland

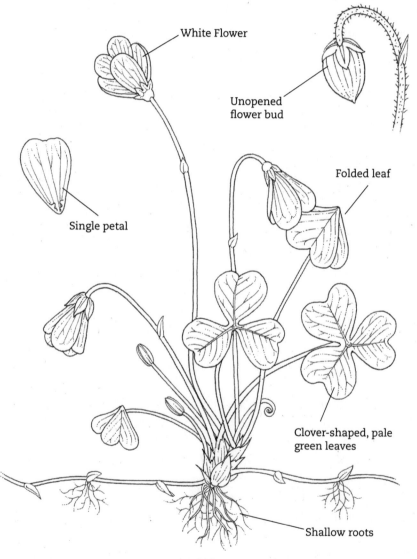

White Flower

Unopened
flower bud

Folded leaf

Single petal

Clover-shaped, pale
green leaves

Shallow roots

How can I recognize Wood Sorrel and where can I find it?

As the name suggests, this little plant belongs in woods – so that's mainly where you will find it. Sometimes you will find it in places that are no longer woodland, but once were. Its distinctive shamrock-like leaves look like a paler-coloured Clover, but somewhat thinner and more delicate. Three heart-shaped leaves emerge from each stem – these are known as a "trefoil" because there are three of them.

At night, or when it starts getting dark, the leaves fold up, and as soon as it is light they open up again.

In the spring and summer, this little plant has pretty white flowers, each with five petals and a little yellow dab of pollen in the centre. If you look closely, you will see that the flowers have lots of lilac veins running through the petals. Like the leaves, the petals fold up when it gets dark and open again the next morning.

Names around the world

French	Oseille des bois
German	Waldsauerklee
Spanish	Aleluya
Welsh	Suran y coed
Polish	Szczawik zajęczy (hare's little sorrel)
Swedish	Harsyra

Your name for this plant:

....

Serving suggestions

Both the flowers and leaves will add a tangy acidic flavour to whatever you serve them with. Their tart flavour is very similar to that of other Sorrels, including the one on p.141. You can use them as a garnish (they are nice floating on top of a smoothie or decorating desserts and cakes), or add them to a salad.

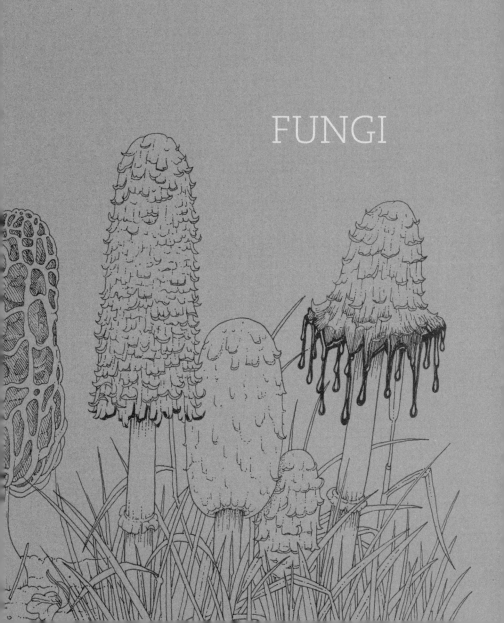

FUNGI

About Fungi

Fungi, mushrooms, toadstools... whatever you care to call them, there are thousands and thousands of these organisms, all of which have a very important part to play in the life of our planet. Some can be seen only with a microscope, but just because they're small that certainly does not mean that they're insignificant.

So, what do fungi do? They can help capture moisture, as well as nutrients, which feed trees and other plants. These trees and plants, in turn, create sugars, which are fed back to the fungi. Also, if you've ever seen fallen trees in woods or forests, you might have wondered how they break down? As well as the wind and the weather, fungi have an important part to play in this process. Although a fallen tree might look dead to you and I, as the timber rots, it provides an essential habitat for different insects and bugs: woodlice, beetles, spiders, wasps and many others. The rotting timber enriches the soil with nutrients, creating a fertile environment for lots of different plants to grow.

WARNING! SOME FUNGI ARE DEADLY POISONOUS. IF YOU ARE NOT 100% CERTAIN OF THE IDENTITY OF A MUSHROOM, DO NOT EAT IT. Check the tree or stump that the fungus is growing on. If you spot a lovely, fresh juicy mushroom (from the ones described here) growing from a yew tree, leave it alone. Yew is very toxic, and the fungus may be affected by the poisonous substances in the tree.

Some fungi give us valuable medicines, such as penicillin. Others encourage a process known as fermentation, which is an important natural effect that results in foods such as Marmite, bread, cheese... and even chocolate! And if you've ever wondered what Quorn™ is made from, you might be surprised to learn that it is also a fungi-based food, often used as a substitute for meat. This fact is extra surprising for people who like Quorn™ but can't stand mushrooms.

As with all wild foods, there is a possibility that you could have an allergy to any of these fungi. Therefore, it's sensible to try just a little at first, properly cooked, to make sure you don't have an adverse reaction.

Of course, some fungi are edible and taste delicious, but others can be very poisonous indeed! This means that you have to be absolutely certain that you're choosing to eat the correct kind. As your confidence as a forager increases, you will learn that the world of fungi is a vast and complex one – a source of lifetime fascination (and often obsession) for many people. This is exactly why I've included some fungi in this book. For your safety, the six mushrooms described here do not resemble any mushroom that might be toxic.

Cauliflower Fungi
Sparassis crispa

Habitat: Woodland

Curly,
cauliflower-like
appearance

Flesh is at its best
when creamy-
white in colour

Cauliflower fungi
often sits on leaf
mould

How can I recognize Cauliflower Fungi and where can I find them?

Also known as the "Wood Cauliflower" or "Cauliflower Mushroom", if you manage to find one of these you really will be surprised and delighted! Seek it in the summer and autumn (fall) months in wooded areas, and look towards the base of pine trees (Scots Pine in particular), which is where it likes to grow.

Names around the world

French	Champignons chou-fleur
German	Krause glucke
Spanish	Seta coliflor
Welsh	Y pengyrch
Polish	Siedzuń sosnowy
Swedish	Blomkålssvamp

Your name for this fungus:

....

The name of this fungi is very appropriate: it looks like a large cauliflower, nestling at the base of the tree. At its best, this fungi is even the same colour as a cauliflower – a creamy white.

As it gets older, though, it blackens and isn't worth eating. It can grow to enormous sizes (up to 40cm/16in across) and, although it feeds from the tree, the fungi doesn't harm its host very much. It can continue to appear in the same place for several years.

And what about that Latin name? The "Sparassis" part means "torn", referring to the irregular tearing pattern which forms the cauliflower-like appearance. You might think that "crispa" would mean a crisp texture, but it actually means "curled" or "waved".

The other bonus about the Cauliflower Fungi is its flavour, which makes it a genuine gourmet delight. Try it in this great twist on cauliflower cheese (see p.152).

Cauliflower Fungi Cheese

Here's a good way to use your Cauliflower Fungi – a twist on a traditional recipe, which uses the fungi in place of the usual cauliflower, topped with a lovely cheese sauce. As with all fungi, make sure that your cauliflower mushroom is young and fresh, and a white or creamy white colour. If it is yellow, and a bit whiffy, you can't eat it. Cauliflower Fungi have lots of small folds where soil and insects can hide, so take time to clean it thoroughly, cutting away any damaged bits.

Serves 4–6

1 cauliflower mushroom, about 20cm (8in) wide, cleaned

50g (1¾oz/3½ tbsp) butter

50g (1¾oz/6 tbsp) plain (all-purpose) flour

1l (35fl oz/4¼ cups) full-fat (whole) milk

160g (5¾oz) strongly-flavoured cheese, such as mature Cheddar, grated

handful of breadcrumbs (optional)

salt and freshly ground black pepper

❶ Preheat the oven to 180°C/350°F/Gas Mark 4.

❷ With a sharp knife, cut the mushroom into large chunks, about 5cm (2in) in size. Place in a baking dish and set aside.

❸ Melt the butter in a large, heavy saucepan over a low heat.

❹ Stir in the flour and cook, stirring, for 2 minutes, making sure that the flour doesn't "catch" on the bottom of the pan.

❺ Take the pan off the heat and add the milk, a little at a time, stirring well between each addition, to make sure the sauce is smooth.

❻ Put the pan back on the heat, stirring all the time, and slowly bring to the boil.

❼ Stir in the cheese and let it melt. Season to taste.

❽ Pour the sauce over the mushrooms in the baking dish, scatter breadcrumbs over the top if you like and season with another grinding of salt and pepper. Bake in the hot oven for 40 minutes, until golden and bubbling.

Chicken of the Woods
Laetiporus sulphureus

Habitat: Woodland

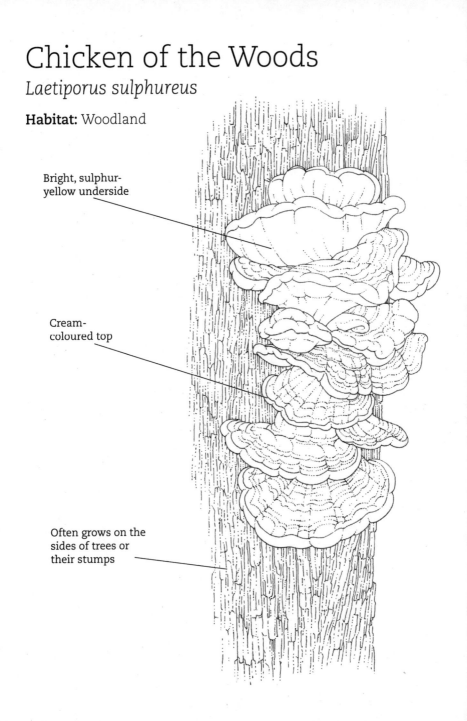

Bright, sulphur-
yellow underside

Cream-
coloured top

Often grows on the
sides of trees or
their stumps

How can I recognize Chicken of the Woods and where can I find it?

This has such an unusual appearance that it can't be mistaken for anything else! It is also one of the tastiest mushrooms you will ever find. Often (but not only) found growing on oak trees, generally in mid- to late-summer, it is a "bracket fungus", comprised of fan-shaped layers with wavy edges (the "shelves" or "brackets"), which are closely stacked together. The brackets can range in size up to 22cm (9in) across. The young surface of this fungi is soft and creamy coloured, with a distinctive bright acid yellow underside, although the colours do fade with time. It can appear on lots of different trees, including oak and willow and, sometimes, conifers.

The name of this particular fungi is very apt: when cooked properly, it not only looks like chicken and has a chicken-like texture, but tastes like it too.

Be sure to pick only fresh young fungi – the older ones tend to be riddled with bugs. If it looks fresh, it will taste really good!

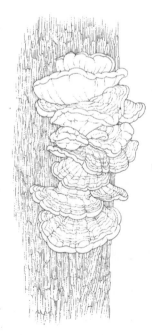

Names around the world

French	Polypore soufre
German	Schwefelporling
Spanish	Poliporo azufrado
Welsh	Ysgwydd felen
Polish	Żółciak siarkowy
Swedish	Svavelticka

Your name for this fungus:

....

Unless you tell people that they're eating a mushroom, it's extremely likely that they will think they are eating chicken! If you prefer, you could make double the amount of smaller, nugget-sized chunks instead of the larger pieces.

Chicken of the Woods in Breadcrumbs

Serves 4

chicken of the woods (about
    8 evenly sized pieces, 15 x 10in
    (6 x 4in) each)
150g (5½oz/2 cups) breadcrumbs
a pinch of paprika (optional)
3 eggs
4 tbsp vegetable oil
50g (1¾oz/3½ tbsp) butter
salt and freshly ground black pepper
chips, salad or rice, to serve

❶ First, wash and dry the mushrooms, cutting off any of the tough parts where it was attached to the bark of the tree.

❷ In a shallow bowl, season the breadcrumbs with salt, pepper and a pinch of paprika (if wished).

❸ Beat the eggs in a separate bowl.

❹ Coat the mushroom pieces in the beaten egg, then toss them in the breadcrumbs, making sure they are thoroughly coated.

❺ Add the oil and butter to a deep frying pan (skillet) or wok over a medium-high heat. When the oil is hot, add the mushroom pieces and fry for about 5 minutes, turning occasionally, until golden brown. Transfer to paper towels to drain, then serve hot, either with chips and a zingy salad, or with rice.

Giant Puffball

Calvatia gigantea

Habitat: Open grassy areas

Fully-grown puffball, creamy-white
in colour

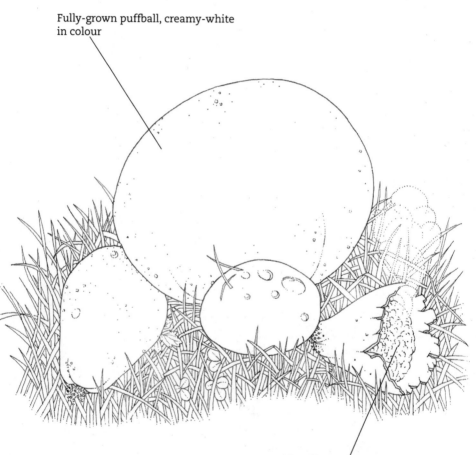

Old puffball releases
powdery, smoky "puffs"
of spores

How can I recognize Giant Puffballs and where can I find them?

When many people see this beauty for the first time, they often mistake it for an abandoned white football lying in the long grass – this is exactly what it looks like!

Generally found in the late summer or early autumn (fall), there may be others dotted around the same area, of varying sizes.

Names around the world

French	Lycoperdon géant
German	Riesenbovist
Spanish	Pedo de lobo gigante
Welsh	Coden fwg (smoke pouch)
Polish	Czasznica olbrzymia
Swedish	Jätteröksvamp

Your name for this fungus:

....

You can find Giant Puffballs in deciduous forests as well as on playing fields and sports pitches.

Pick it up, turn it upside down and you'll see the place where the fungi was attached to the earth, marked by a slightly puckered skin which is usually has some soil attached. Giant Puffballs can range from 10–70cm (4–27in) in diameter, hence their name!

As fungi go, this also ranks as one of the tastiest.

Young puffball flesh should be firm and white all the way through. If there is any kind of yellowish colouring when you cut into it, then the puffball has passed its sell-by-date and is not fit to eat. Don't throw it away, though – put it back where you found it, or in similar conditions, to give the spores a chance to grow again next year.

Giant Puffball "Steaks"

This is the easiest and simplest recipe for your delicious harvest of Giant Puffball. You'll notice that cutting it with a serrated bread knife make little stripes in the flesh of the puffball, which make the slices look just like steaks! Serve with a wild side salad and buttery mashed potatoes.

Serves 4–6

1 giant puffball, cleaned of any soil
oil, for frying
1 tbsp butter
1–2 garlic cloves, crushed (or more to taste)
dash of soy sauce

❶ Use a serrated bread knife (the kind with little teeth all down the blade) to cut the puffball into slices, about 6mm (¼in) thick.

❷ Heat the oil and butter in a frying pan (skillet) over a medium heat. Add crushed garlic to taste and a decent dash of soy sauce. When the garlic begins to sizzle, add as many slices of puffball as will fit in the pan and cook for 2–3 minutes, then use a spatula to carefully turn them over. Cook for a further 2–3 minutes, or until browned. If necessary, heap the slices onto a plate to keep warm in a low oven while you cook the rest (you may need to add more oil to the pan).

Morel

Morchella esculenta

Habitat: At the edges of forests, often in amongst bark chippings; near oak or ash trees; gravelly places

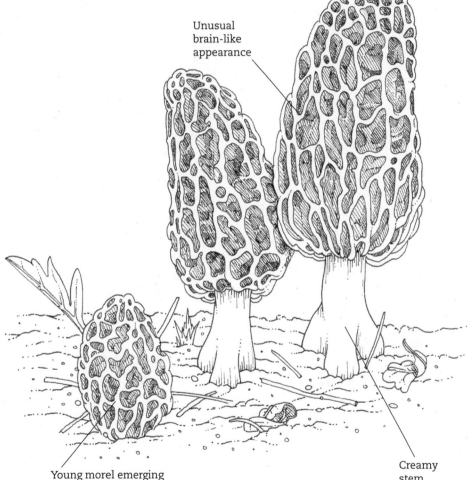

Unusual brain-like appearance

Young morel emerging from ground

Creamy stem

How can I recognize Morels and where can I find them?

Morels are one of the most easily identified, as well as one of the most sought-after fungi, since they are so delicious. They have a very distinctive appearance – in short, they look like an elongated brain on a stem, or a bit like a loofah sponge, growing to a height of up to 10cm (4in).

If you decide to go looking for them, try searching in areas of deciduous woodland, as well as in gardens, patches of scorched ground, old orchards, heaps of rotting wood and discarded woodchips, and even gravel.

Although morels are more likely to appear in the early spring, they don't always follow this pattern. The best advice is simply to keep your eyes peeled and you might get lucky.

Serving suggestion

These particular mushrooms are highly valued by the very best chefs in the world, so if you do find some, you simply must eat them. Do what the chefs do and fry the fresh Morels in butter with a little sea salt and cracked black pepper. That's all you need to do – delicious on toast!

As with most mushrooms, they are best not eaten raw since this can cause an upset stomach.

Names around the world

French Morille
German Morchel
Spanish Colmenillas
Welsh Morel
Polish Smardz
Swedish Toppmurkla
Your name for this fungus:

....

Scarlet Elf Cup

Sarcoscypha coccinea

Habitat: Fallen sticks and logs in damp, shady woodland

Hollow "cup" shape

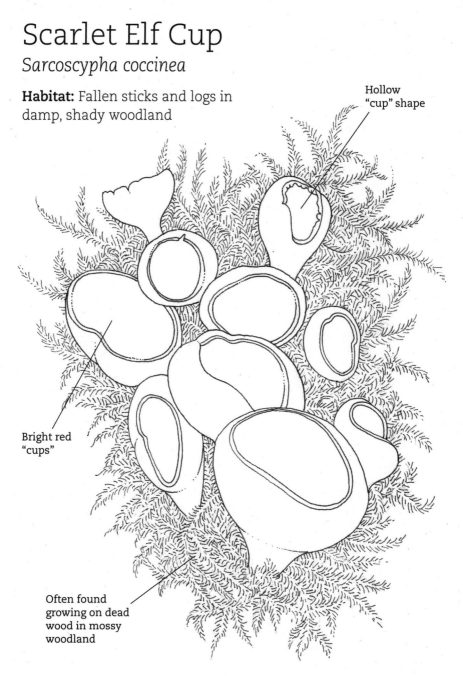

Bright red "cups"

Often found growing on dead wood in mossy woodland

How can I recognize Scarlet Elf Cups and where can I find them?

These beautiful little fungi are bright red. Since they grow in damp woods during the winter months, when there's not much else around, they are easy to spot due to their vivid colour. Scarlet Elf Cups range in size from 1–4cm (⅜–1½in) in diameter. The top is scarlet-coloured and shaped exactly as you would expect, like a little bowl. If you look underneath, at the back of the mushroom, you will see that it has a short tapering stem that is a pale orangey colour.

Names around the world

French   Tasses d'elfes écarlates

German   Scharlach elf tassen

Spanish   Copas de elfo escarlata

Welsh   Cwpan Robin goch

Polish   Czarka szkarłatna

Swedish   Scharlakansvårskå

Your name for this fungus:

....

Sautéed Elf Cups

Sautéing brings out the flavour of this mushroom. Cooked in this way they make a lovely garnish, or, if you have enough of them, serve on a slice of toast, seasoned to taste.

Before cooking, simply brush away any soil, rinse in water and pat dry with absorbent paper towels.

Serves 4

1 tbsp butter

oil for frying

1–2 garlic cloves, crushed

40 scarlet elf cups (10 per person), cleaned

salt and freshly ground black pepper to taste

❶ Melt the butter and a little oil in a frying pan (skillet) set over a low heat, then add the crushed garlic. Cook for 2 minutes, then add the mushrooms. You don't need to fry them for long: 5–8 minutes should do it. Season to taste before serving.

Shaggy Ink Cap
Coprinus comatus

Habitat: Woodland, verges, rough grassland

Soft "scaly" older skin

Black inky drips

Young, creamy white skin

Young Ink Cap about to emerge

How can I recognize Shaggy Ink Caps and where can I find them?

Also known as "Lawyer's Wig" or "Shaggy Mane", the Shaggy Ink Cap is generally easy to spot since it is very distinctive. It grows to about 15cm (6in) tall, has a long stem and, initially, an elongated bell-shaped "cap", which gradually opens out, the edges curling up to reveal blackish edges that drip an inky black liquid onto the ground below. These fungi are best eaten before the cap has opened up. After a few days, the inky bits melt away leaving just the stem.

You'll find it at the edges of woods, on verges and in areas of rough grassland. I've even seen it coming up through the gravel at the edges of a car park! It also thrives in areas that have been grazed by cows, sheep or pigs: the Latin name "Coprinus" means "living on dung". Don't let this put you off – manure of all kinds is beneficial to plants, since it provides an effective form of nutrition for the soil. The other part of the name, "comatus" means "hairy" and refers to the shaggy scales that feather the sides and edges of this particular fungus.

Names around the world

French	Capuchon d'encre
German	Schopf-Tintling
Spanish	Barbuda o matacandil
Welsh	Cap du blewog
Polish	Czernidłak kołpakowaty
Swedish	Fjällig bläcksvamp

Your name for this fungus:

....

Ink Caps are often found in colonies, which means you can gather quite a few. Make sure that the ones you gather are young and firm, and have not started to open up too much. The best time to find them is in the spring or autumn (fall). They tend to stay in the same place, so make a note of their location for future reference.

Serving suggestion

Eat them as soon as you can: even keeping them in the fridge overnight will mean they will have passed their best by morning. Simply fry them in oil and butter, with a little bit of garlic and perhaps a hint of chilli powder, and either serve on toast or chop finely and add to a soup or stew.

GARLIC,
ONION &
MUSTARD

Garlic, Onion or Mustard

As your interest in foraging increases, so will your knowledge. But sometimes, working things out can take quite a while. It took me a long time to realize just how many plants have a lemony, citrusy taste (think of tart Apples, Lemon Sorrel or Wood Sorrel). It also took a long time before it dawned on me that another large group of plants taste very much like garlic, onions or mustard – or in some cases, all three. So in grouping these plants together, I hope I've given you a bit of a short cut!

The plants that taste like garlic or onion will generally belong to the Allium family. These include "ordinary" garlic, as well as Wild Garlic, leeks, onions, shallots and chives.

The plants that taste like mustard will generally belong to the Brassica family (or Brassicaceae or even Cruciferae – this last word is Latin and means "cross-bearing". It refers to the flowers belonging to the group, each of which has four symmetrical petals that look like a little cross). As well as Hairy Bittercress and Wintercress, other brassicas include cabbage, kale, broccoli, choi sum, pak choi, turnips and, of course, mustard.

The leaves of all these plants have a powerful flavour; sometimes, it can take a little while to get used to the taste. It's worth persevering, though, since your taste buds change as you get older. I made a meal recently that included the sauce made with Jack-by-the-Hedge (see p.173). A friend loved the sauce enough to ask for the recipe. She was astonished when she found out what was in it, as some time ago she had decided that she didn't like either garlic OR mustard, and yet she'd just wiped her plate clean to mop up the very last drop of a sauce that tasted of both! Now she knows that she loves these flavours, it means that she has more choice, both in her home-cooking as well as when she goes out to eat. Little things like this can change your life for the better!

Crow Garlic
Allium vineale

Habitat: Dry, poor soil, as well as verges, tracks and pathways

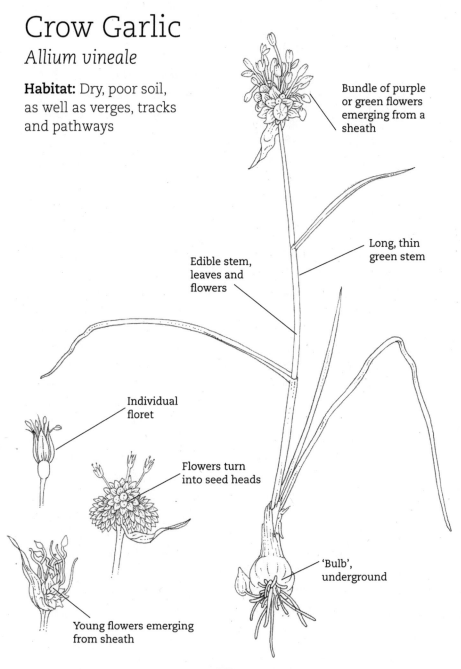

Bundle of purple or green flowers emerging from a sheath

Long, thin green stem

Edible stem, leaves and flowers

Individual floret

Flowers turn into seed heads

Young flowers emerging from sheath

'Bulb', underground

How can I recognize Crow Garlic and where can I find it?

Also known as Wild Onion, Crow Garlic is a tall plant, growing up to 80cm (2½ft) high. In the early spring, you may see long, thin green strands emerging from the earth, which look like a thick, dark green grass (they also look very similar to Chives, often grown as a garden herb). It flowers during the summer months. The tall flower stems are topped by a flower head, like a drumstick, which gradually gets bigger until it starts to bulge, then bursts opens to reveal lots of tiny purple or green flowers; this is a typical onion-shaped flower, and one that you might recognize if you have ever seen ornamental Alliums in peoples' gardens.

Crow Garlic will grow along verges, in sandy places, in quite dry grassland where the soil hasn't been enriched, and even in rocky places. Unlike Ramsons (see p.180), Crow Garlic doesn't favour damp, shady places. For many people, the plant becomes a bit of a pest; those tiny flowers, called bulbils, drop to the ground and turn into more plants.

Names around the world

French	Ail de vignes
German	Weinbergs-lauch
Spanish	Ajo salvaje
Welsh	Garlleg Mair (Mary's garlic)
Polish	Czosnek winnicowy (vineyard garlic)
Swedish	Sandlök

Your name for this plant:

....

Serving suggestions

All parts of this plant are edible – the leaves, the stems, the flowers and even the seeds. The leaves and stems are great in a soup or a salad, or can be used to make a pesto (see p.179). You can also blitz them in a blender and mash into softened butter to make a garlic butter (great on baked potatoes). The flowers make a delicious edible garnish, and the fresh seeds can be sprinkled anywhere that you would like a crunchy, garlicky flavour and texture – in a cream cheese sandwich, for instance.

Hairy Bittercress
Cardamine hirsuta

Habitat: On soil that has been disturbed

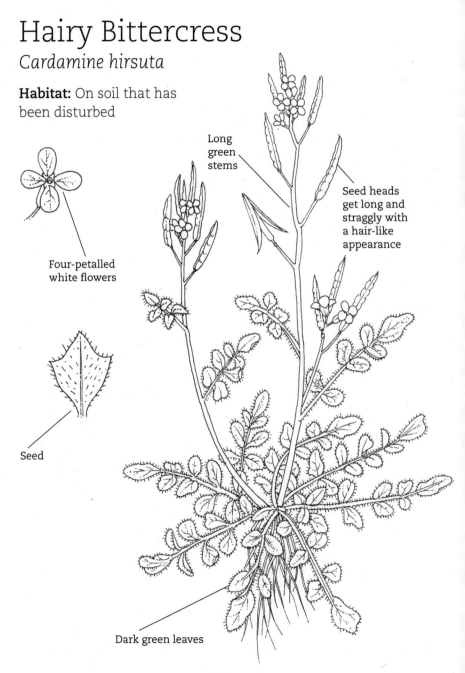

Long green stems

Seed heads get long and straggly with a hair-like appearance

Four-petalled white flowers

Seed

Dark green leaves

"Cardamine" is the word for "cress"; "hirsuta" means "hairy". This plant is not really bitter, but it does have the sharp mustardy tang that you would expect from a cress. Secondly, it isn't hairy, although as the plant ages the long seed heads do appear to look like greenish strands of hair. Once the plant is looking stringy like this, it's too tough to eat.

Originating in both Europe and Asia, this smart little plant has made itself at home all over the world, carried by humans, or animals, or insects, or the wind. It goes by many different names, including: Land Cress, Hoary Bittercress, Spring Cress, Shotweed and Flickweed (these last two are because the tiny seed heads pop when ripe and shower seeds everywhere!).

How can I recognize Hairy Bittercress and where can I find it?

Hairy Bittercress grows up to 30cm (12in) high. It has small white flowers, each with four petals, often with a lilac blush. These four petals are typical of all cress-related plants (which belong to the same family as cabbages).

Names around the world

French	Cardamine herissée
German	Behaartes schaumkraut
Spanish	Mastuerzo amargo
Welsh	Berw chwerw (bitter berries)
Polish	Rzeżucha włochata
Swedish	Bergbråsma

Your name for this plant:

....

Hairy Bittercress likes to seed itself in soil that has been turned over fresh for planting. Gardeners who have no idea how tasty it is can get annoyed when faced with a fresh growth of the keen young plants. It is easy to uproot, but if they knew how nice it is to eat, they would definitely not put it in the compost bin!

Serving suggestion
Luckily for us foragers, Hairy Bittercress tastes lovely. Try the fresh young leaves sprinkled over buttery mashed potato, or maybe in an egg sandwich instead of "normal" cress. A bonus is that this little plant is full of vitamin C... and costs nothing!

Jack-by-the-Hedge
Alliaria petiolata

Habitat: Hedgerows, wasteland

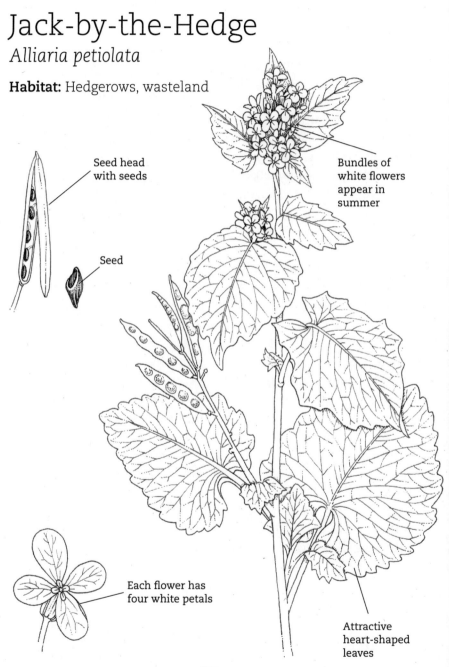

Seed head
with seeds

Seed

Bundles of
white flowers
appear in
summer

Each flower has
four white petals

Attractive
heart-shaped
leaves

"Alliaria" means "like allium" ("Allium" is the name for the family of plants that includes all kinds of onions, including garlic). This plant smells like garlic when crushed, but it's actually a member of the mustard family of plants. "Petiolata" simply means the leaves have stalks.

As for the plant's common name, the "by-the-hedge" part is obvious, coming from where you'll find it growing, and I was once told that "Jack" is an old name for the devil, which probably refers to the sharp, tangy garlic flavour left in your mouth when you chew on a leaf. I have no way of knowing whether this is true! Another reason for the name might be that the plant is very common, and the name "Jack" was once very common too, referring to any boy or man.

Jack-by-the-Hedge has lots of other names, too, which tells us that it was once well-loved.

It's also called Garlic Mustard, Jack-in-the-Bush, Hedge Garlic, Penny Hedge, Garlic Root (the roots also smell and taste strongly

Names around the world	
French	Alliaire
German	Knoblauchsrauke
Spanish	Hierba de ajo
Welsh	Garllegog Troed yr Asen (donkey's foot garlic)
Polish	Czosnaczek pospolity
Swedish	Löktrav

Your name for this plant:

....

of garlic) and Sauce Plant (this is because the leaves were once used to make a sauce, which in the UK and US, was traditionally eaten with salted meats).

How can I recognize Jack-by-the-Hedge and where can I find it?

As you'd expect from the name, this plant is often found in hedgerows, as well as at the edges of fields and on waste ground.

Jack-by-the-Hedge takes two years to become fully grown. In its first year, it appears as a clumpy rosette of leaves, each of them the shape of a heart with a finely serrated edge, carried on skinny stalks. In its second year, it will grow up to 1m (3ft) tall. The leaves at the bottom of the plant can get quite large, slightly bigger than an adult person's hand, while the leaves get smaller towards the top of the plant, which makes an attractive spire shape. In late spring and early summer you'll see small clusters (about 2–3cm (1in) wide) of tiny white flowers, each with four petals. Later, the flowers are replaced by long stick-like seed pods, the preferred food of the caterpillar of the Orange-Tip Butterfly.

The definitive way to recognize Jack-by-the-Hedge, though, is by its scent. Take one of the leaves and crush it between your fingers, then sniff – you will get the unmistakeable scent of onions, garlic or mustard.

If you don't like the flavour of any of these, then it's unlikely that you will like the taste of the raw leaves! Try them anyway. As we grow, our taste buds change; often something which seems horrible the first time you try it can be surprisingly delicious the next time.

Serving suggestions

The raw leaves used to be regularly used in salads – try them the same way, using a mixture of different leaves and a little oil, vinegar and lemon juice to dress them.

The recipe on p.176 uses a simple Jack-by-the-Hedge sauce as a dressing for pasta. Other uses? How about steaming it as a topping for baked potatoes, or combining it with yogurt to make a dip for nachos, or mixing it with olive oil for a salad dressing? Use your imagination!

Since one of the old names for Jack-by-the-Hedge is Sauce Plant, I thought it would be fun to make a sauce to go with pasta!

Tagliatelle with Jack-by-the-Hedge Sauce

Serves 4

4 good handfuls jack-by-the-hedge leaves, stalks removed
1 knob of butter
dash of oil
1 large onion, finely chopped
4 garlic cloves, crushed
500g (18oz/2 cups) cream cheese
300g (10½oz) tagliatelle
salt and freshly ground black pepper, to taste
1 handful toasted pine nuts, to serve

❶ Bring a large saucepan of salted water to the boil. Wash and drain the jack-by-the-hedge leaves and add to the pan. Cook for just 1 minute to tenderize the leaves, then drain in a colander and leave to cool and drip-dry.

❷ Heat the butter and oil in a large frying pan (skillet) over a low heat. Add the onion and cook for 3–4 minutes, stirring, then add the garlic and cook for a further 1–2 minutes, until tender and golden. Remove from the heat.

❸ Take the jack-by-the-hedge leaves and squeeze as much water out of them as you can. Chop them roughly, then whizz in a blender until smooth. Add the cooked onions and garlic, cream cheese, and some salt and pepper and whizz once more, until blended and silky smooth.

❹ Cook the tagliatelle in a large saucepan of boiling water, according to the packet directions, until just al dente. Dried tagliatelle will take about 10 minutes; fresh tagliatelle will take 3–5 minutes. (One fun way of checking to see whether it is cooked, is to throw a piece at the ceiling – if it sticks, then it's done. However, do ask for permission before hurling pasta at the kitchen ceiling!)

❺ Drain the tagliatelle and transfer to a large serving bowl, then stir in the sauce (you might prefer not to use all of it). Sprinkle the pine nuts over the top and serve.

Three-cornered Leek or Three-cornered Garlic

Allium triquetrum

Habitat: Hedgerows, verges, edges of fields and open woodland

White six-petalled flowers

Drooping flowers, similar to snowdrops

Three-sided stem

Narrow, strap-like leaves

How can I recognize Three-cornered Leek and where can I find it?

Yet another sort of Wild Garlic, this plant grows up to 60cm (2ft) tall, with long, narrow stems that have three sides (hence the name). In the spring, it produces little drooping bunches of up to 18 bell-shaped flowers, which look a little like large snowdrops; white with green stripes. It is not uncommon for people to mistake this plant for a white bluebell or a large snowdrop (please note that snowdrops are not edible). The tell-tale way to identify this plant is by its pungent onion/garlic scent.

Three-cornered Leek originated in the Mediterranean, but has spread all over the world. It likes to grow at the edges of fields, in hedges, in dry-ish soil, in open woodland, and also in sandy areas.

Names around the world

French	Ail triquètre
German	Dreikantiger Lauch
Spanish	Lágrimas de la Virgen
Welsh	no Welsh name
Polish	Czosnek niedźwiedzi
Swedish	Sloklök

Your name for this plant:

....

Serving suggestions

All parts of the plant are edible. Of the three garlics mentioned in this chapter, the Three-cornered Leek has the mildest flavour; less "spiky" than some of the others (more like a leek, as the names suggests). It is sweet enough to eat raw in salads or as a sandwich filling.

See also the Wild Garlic Pesto recipe on p.179.

Wild Garlic Pesto

All three kinds of Wild Garlic make an absolutely delicious pesto, which can be used in exactly the same way that you would use a "normal" pesto – dollop heaps of it onto pasta for a scrummy dinner. It's ridiculously easy to make! You can make it with any of the garlics mentioned here, or you could also add some Jack-by-the-Hedge (see p.173) to give it even more of a kick, or maybe some Ground Elder (see p.107) for a cooler flavour.

Makes 200g (7 oz/1 cup)

100g (3½oz) wild garlic leaves (or stems, flowers or seeds), washed and patted dry with paper towels

50g (2oz) strong, hard cheese, such as Cheddar or Parmesan, finely grated

50g (2oz/⅓ cup) toasted pine nuts (optional)

1 tbsp olive oil (optional)

salt and freshly ground black pepper, to taste

❶ Simply put all the ingredients, except the olive oil, into a blender or food processor and blitz to preferred consistency (or grind in a pestle and mortar). You will find that so much juice comes from the leaves that you don't need to add oil.

❷ If you're not planning on using your pesto immediately, transfer it to a sterilized jar or airtight container (see p.222) and pour the olive oil over the top to preserve it. It will keep unopened in the refrigerator for up to a week. Once opened, use immediately.

Ramsons

Allium ursinum

Habitat: Damp, shady places, woodland

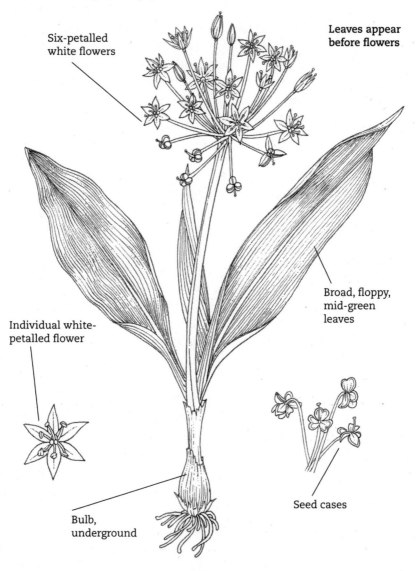

Six-petalled
white flowers

Leaves appear
before flowers

Broad, floppy,
mid-green
leaves

Individual white-
petalled flower

Bulb,
underground

Seed cases

How do I recognize Ramsons and where can I find them?

Although you may think you have never have encountered Ramsons, it's likely they will be growing closer than you think. Often (but not always) a plant of ancient woodlands, this kind of wild garlic can be found near streams, bluebells, wood anemones and shade. They also grow along roadside verges.

The tips of the leaves start to appear in the very early spring; bright little spears popping up through the leaf litter of the winter. As they grow up to 30cm (1ft) long, the leaves, elegantly tapered at both ends, get floppier; at this stage you can smell the strong garlic scent of the leaves if you happen to be treading on them. The flowers start to show themselves on long stalks later in spring, shiny white stars bobbing in the dense greenery. Once the flowers are open you can smell the wild garlic from some distance away, although when they appear the leaves will soon start to die back. The good news is that the flowers are edible, as are the seeds, which appear after the flowers.

Names around the world

French Ail des ours
German Bärlauch
Spanish Ajo de oso
Welsh Garlleg yr arth (bear's garlic)
Polish Czosnek niedźwiedzi
Swedish Ramslök
Your name for this plant:

....

A NOTE OF CAUTION: the leaves of this particular garlic look very like those of two other plants – Lily of the Valley (not seen very often in the wild these days, it's more popular in gardens) and Lords and Ladies, which is very common indeed. Both of these plants are poisonous. Lily of the Valley develops small white flowers, a bit like those belonging to hyacinths. Lords and Ladies often has mottled leaves, and the leaves get much wider than those of the garlic. Luckily, the scent of wild garlic will tell you what it is; the other two plants don't smell anything like it at all.

If you're gathering your Ramsons in ancient woodland, then it is probable that the plant has been growing there for thousands of years. And it is also likely that generations of people have crouched exactly where you are, in the same footsteps, picking this rich harvest.

This thought always gives me a little tingle. Plants, you may start to find, are like a sort of living archaeology.

Incidentally, "normal" garlic – the knobbly white bulb of lots of little wedge-shaped cloves wrapped up in papery skin, that you've probably got in your kitchen – is a close relative of Wild Garlic. While we can peel and crush the bulb of ordinary garlic to use in our cooking, Ramsons do not have much of a bulb at all. However, the stalks, leaves, flowers and seeds are not only all edible, but are all delicious.

Serving suggestions

The intensely garlicky/oniony flavour of Ramsons is one that many people are surprised by. If you love it, you will enjoy tearing up the leaves into salads or sandwiches, using them in a soup (they work very well with a simple leek and potato recipe) or stirring them into pasta just before serving. How about including them in an omelette?

You can use the flowers as a garnish for salads or hot dishes – they taste and look great!

Try scattering the green seeds over the top of a loaf of home-baked bread before baking – they will add both crunch and flavour.

See also the Wild Garlic Pesto recipe on p.179.

Wintercress

Barbarea vulgaris

Habitat: Damp, disburbed earth, such as at the edge of streams, ditches, wasteland and verges

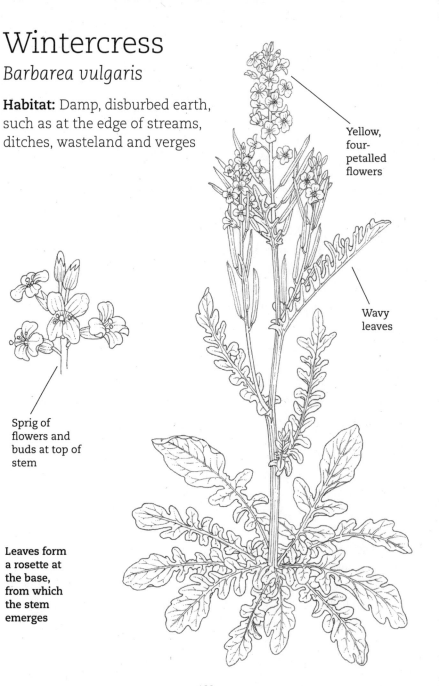

Yellow, four-petalled flowers

Wavy leaves

Sprig of flowers and buds at top of stem

Leaves form a rosette at the base, from which the stem emerges

Wintercress is relatively common but is also often ignored, for some reason. A member of the cabbage family, it appears in the winter months, as the name suggests, when other leafy vegetables can be scarce.

Wintercress is named for St Barbara, an early Christian martyr, whose saint day is on 4 December, by which time the plants are out and about, doing their thing. (Amongst other things, St Barbara is the patron saint of both mathematicians and people who work with explosives!) It is also called Yellow Rocket.

How do I recognize Wintercress and where can I find it?

The leaves of Wintercress look very like the leaves of Hairy Bittercress (p.171), except much larger. This plant will grow up to 1m (3ft) tall; the stems long and smooth. The young plant appears as a rosette of leaves, lying flat on the ground, then starts to get bushier, before sending up a central shoot bearing lots of side shoots. These side shoots bear small bunches of yellow flowers, each with four petals.

Names around the world

French	Barbarée
German	Winterkresse
Spanish	Hierba de Santa Bárbara
Welsh	Berwr Caersalem
Polish	Gorczycznik pospolity
Swedish	Sommargyllen

Your name for this plant:

....

Wintercress pops up in lots of locations, such as wasteland and verges, but prefers damper spots and places where the soil is disturbed stream edges and ditches provide such a habitat.

Serving suggestions

Use Wintercress in the same way that you would use cabbage – the leaves, stems and flowers are all edible. It has a peppery taste and a nice firm texture.

Once the flowers start to appear, the leaves and stalks can get tough. You can pick the unopened flower heads and steam them – they taste very good with a dressing such as béarnaise sauce.

Wintercress Slaw

This recipe is very simple, requiring no cooking. We like to serve it with pizza!

Serves 6, as a side dish

100g (3½oz/scant ½ cup) plain yogurt
juice of ½ lemon
1 tbsp wholegrain mustard
¼ small white cabbage, finely shredded
¼ small red cabbage, finely shredded
1 small red onion, finely shredded
½ small cucumber, finely sliced
sea salt and freshly ground black pepper, to taste
3 tbsp chopped wintercress leaves and flowers

❶ Combine the yogurt, lemon juice and mustard in a large bowl, then add all the remaining ingredients, except the wintercress. Stir together until thoroughly combined. Leave at room temperature for at least 30 minutes before serving, to let the flavours blend. Just before serving, stir in the wintercress.

TREES

About Trees

I really wanted to include trees as a category in this book. In fact, the scope for foraging from trees – and trees alone – is so huge that one day I want to write a book just about them!

Including trees in this book is also a reminder that foraging is not just about looking down. It's also about looking up! Having said that, it's on the ground that you will often find the fruits, nuts and seeds that belong to trees, even when the tree itself might be some distance away. For example, there's a large churchyard fairly close to where I live. Recently, I noticed quite a few chestnuts on the ground, but no sign of the actual tree anywhere close by. Later, I found the tree about 30 metres/100 feet away, in a large garden. The nuts hadn't been taken by squirrels because they were intact. They must have either bounced all that way, or been blown by the wind.

For mankind, trees are possibly one of the most important aspects of the natural world. We build houses and boats from trees. We use trees to heat those houses. Just take a look around your own home – how many things can you see that are made of wood? Furniture, shelving, doors, the floor, picture frames, coathangers, cupboard handles. How about pencils? Even cardboard and paper, so common that we hardly notice them, are made from wood pulp.

As trees are our among our largest and most long-lived plants, it stands to reason that we can get very fond of particular specimens, which may have formed a part of the landscape for hundreds, if not thousands, of years. Most days, I walk my dogs through a field called Maes Derwen, which means "field of the oaks". One of the oak trees in this field is reputed to be at least 500 years old. And when I forage for Wild Garlic, it's in a stretch of ancient woodland full of oak, ash and beech trees. The trees there make me feel a very real connection to the people that foraged for Wild Garlic several centuries ago, beneath the same trees. The more often you go out foraging, the more and more you will realize that it's not just about gathering edible plants!

Horse Chestnut Tree
Aescalus hippocastanum

Habitat: Large parks and gardens,
field edges and verges

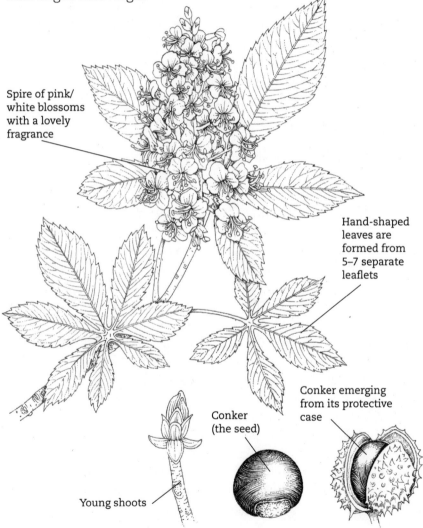

Spire of pink/
white blossoms
with a lovely
fragrance

Hand-shaped
leaves are
formed from
5–7 separate
leaflets

Conker emerging
from its protective
case

Conker
(the seed)

Young shoots

The "hippo" part of the name means "horse", and although there are theories about the plant having once been used as a medicine for horses, there is little evidence to tell us that this is actually true. N.B. This entry is the odd one out in the book, because this tree itself is NOT edible! So why is it included? Keep reading below to find out why.

Names around the world

French Marronnier

German Rosskastanie

Spanish Castaño de Indias

Welsh Castanwydden y meirch

Polish Kasztanowiec zwyczajny, Kasztan

Swedish Hästkastanj

Your name for this plant:

....

How can I recognize a Horse Chestnut Tree and where can I find one?

A fully-grown Horse Chestnut Tree can be up to 40m (130ft) tall, which can make a huge impact on the landscape. As I'm writing, I can see one right across from my desk, just outside. "My" Horse Chestnut Tree is known to be 80 years old; hopefully it will live for another 220 years. Since I'm writing this book in the winter, and the tree is deciduous, all its leaves have fallen and I'm looking at the bare silhouette. The leaves of this particular tree are very distinctive, looking a bit like a hand, with five–seven separate leaves emerging from the same stem in a fan shape.

The blossoms, which start to appear mid-spring, are very beautiful – a spire of pink or white flowers about 10cm (4in) long. These flowers have a wonderful, otherworldly scent, which seems to be more noticeable in the late afternoon/early evening. The caterpillars of various moths, including the Horse-Chestnut Leaf-Miner moth, feed on these flowers. Blue Tits, in turn, feed on the caterpillars.

In the late summer to early autumn (fall), the seeds of the Horse Chestnut – commonly called "conkers" – appear.

These seeds are glossy brown and hard, up to 4cm (1½in) in diameter, and emerge from spiky green casings. Conkers are NOT edible. The reasons I've decided to include the Horse Chestnut Tree are because if you've never played a game of conkers, you're missing out! First, select a decent conker. With the help of an adult, drill a hole through the middle (top to bottom) with a thin knitting needle. Push an old shoelace through the hole and tie a big, bobbly knot at one end to stop the conker falling off. Get a friend to do the same thing, then you can enjoy the age-old tradition of swipes at each other's conker. The first conker to get smashed up is the loser.

TOP TIP – There are several methods believed to make your conker harder and more lethal, including soaking in vinegar or baking in a low oven. Try them and see.

Also, Conkers make good soap. In fact, an old name for them is "soapnuts". Some very expensive bath products still use conkers as an important ingredient – look for products with pictures of Horse Chestnut leaves or conkers on the packaging. A plant that makes soap is called "saponaceous". There's a recipe for how to make conker soap on p.192.

WARNING – Any game that involves flinging about small hard objects tied to a piece of string could potentially hurt, especially if that small hard object hits you on the nose or in the eye. So, do take care.

This "recipe" cleverly uses silicone cupcake cases as moulds to make bars of soap. You can use it just as you would normal soap, or pop it into the bath and stir around, letting it dissolve like a bath tablet.

Conker Soap

Makes about 2 bars (depending on the size of your mould)

30 conkers

❶ Using a potato peeler, carefully peel the shiny outer shell away from each conker. Grate the white interior part of the conkers (mind your fingers).

❷ Fill a bowl with warm water, then put a clean J-cloth (dish cloth) over the bowl, pushing the cloth down so that it touches the bottom of the bowl, with the rest of the cloth draped over the sides of the bowl. Put the grated conkers into the water and leave them to soak for 2 hours.

❸ Gather together the edges of the J-cloth to form a bag and pull the cloth (with the grated conkers inside) out of the water. Squeeze out as much water as you can. Pack the conker gratings into 1 or 2 silicone cupcake cases, pressing them firmly into the moulds. Pour away any excess water that you manage to further squeeze out (you'll find that your hands feel very soft).

❹ Set the moulds aside to dry out for a day or two, then turn the "soap" out of the moulds. You can wrap it in wax paper to keep it, but when made in this way, your lovely homemade soap doesn't have a very long shelf-life, so use it within a couple of weeks.

Douglas Fir Tree
Pseudotsuga menziesii

Habitat: Forestry plantations, large gardens, country parks

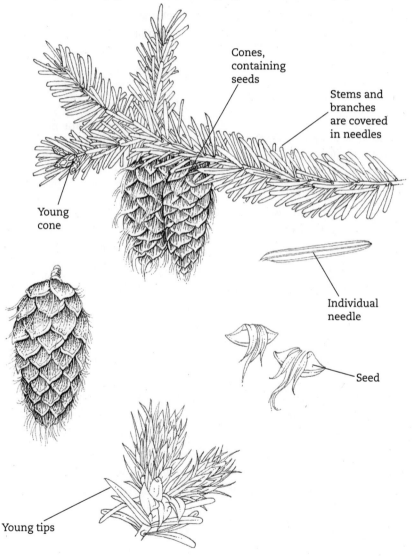

Cones, containing seeds

Stems and branches are covered in needles

Young cone

Individual needle

Young tips

Seed

The Douglas Fir originates from the west coast of North America, and so it is sometimes called the Oregon Pine (Oregon is a state in that part of the world). It is called the Douglas Fir after the plant gatherer who first discovered it; David Douglas was born in Scotland in 1799, and died in Hawaii only 35 years later.

Although I've chosen the Douglas Fir to include here, any pine, fir or spruce tree is edible. Whilst it would be impossible to eat an entire tree at once (only joking), the needles of any of these trees taste really lovely when ground up with sugar – you can use the powder as a sprinkle over the top of a Christmas cake or over mince pies. A ratio of 50/50 needles to granulated sugar usually tastes about right, ground very finely in a blender.

How can I recognize a Douglas Fir Tree and where can I find one?

The Douglas Fir is often used as a decorative tree in parks and large gardens. It can reach 100m (330ft) in height, so it needs lots of space to grow! This is an evergreen tree with needle-like "leaves" and

> ### Names around the world
>
> **French** Douglas Vert, Sapin de Douglas
>
> **German** Douglastanne
>
> **Spanish** Pino Oregón
>
> **Welsh** Ffynidwydden Douglas
>
> **Polish** Daglezja zielona, Jedlica zielona
>
> **Swedish** Douglasgran
>
> **Your name for this plant:**
>
> ....

long cones, up to 10cm (4in) long. Mainly, you will see the tree if you head up to an area of forestry, where the trees have been planted to be harvested (as you know, trees are useful for making lots of things, such as furniture and paper).

Tear a little piece of stem from a Douglas Fir and have a sniff of the "juice". The scent is immediately refreshing, a bit like a drink of cold water for your nose (this is probably why so many air fresheners use an artificial pine fragrance). The real thing, in case you're concerned, does not smell like toilet cleaner – it smells so much nicer.

Pine-Needle Lemonade

This is a refreshingly unusual drink, which – I'd guess – few of your friends will have tried before. See if they can guess what it is!

Makes 1.5l (52fl oz/6½ cups)

juice of 3 lemons (or a mixture of lemons and limes)

150ml (5fl oz/⅔ cup) maple syrup

1.25l (40fl oz/5 cups) hot water

2 fresh young pine tips (can be from any spruce, pine or fir tree)

ice, to serve

❶ Put the lemon/lime juice in a jug, add the maple syrup and hot water and whisk to combine. Pour into two sterilized 750-ml (26-fl oz) bottles with lids (see p.222).

❷ Allow to cool, then add the young pine, spruce or fir tips. Leave to infuse for at least 3 hours, then serve over ice. It will keep for up to 2 weeks in the refrigerator.

Sweet Chestnut Tree

Castanea sativa

Habitat: Parks, fields, large gardens

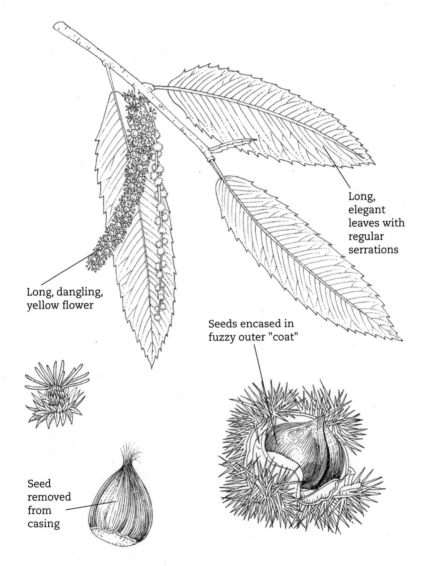

Long, elegant leaves with regular serrations

Long, dangling, yellow flower

Seeds encased in fuzzy outer "coat"

Seed removed from casing

The Sweet Chestnut is not to be confused with the Horse Chestnut, which is not edible (see p.189). These two trees look very different, as do their fruits, but for some reason people do confuse them, probably because of the "chestnut" part of the name.

The word "sativa" refers to plants that people have cultivated to eat. Also, if you've ever visited Spain or seen a flamenco dance show, you might have noticed a small percussion instrument held in the hands of the dancers, which is used to make a "clicketty clack" beat. These are called castanets, which are traditionally made from the wood of this tree.

How can I recognize a Sweet Chestnut Tree and where can I find one?

Sweet Chestnut Trees are often planted in city parks or in the grounds of stately homes, and can also be found in fields and large gardens. A fully-grown Sweet Chestnut can reach 35m (115ft). It has dark green, glossy, lance-shaped leaves with little saw-toothed serrations, hanging in bunches from the branches. In spring and summer you'll see the flowers – long dangling yellow blossoms. Later in the year come the parts of the tree that are edible – the nuts. These are protected by a green, fuzzy, prickly outer case, which splits into four to reveal a collection of two–three nuts, generally with one nut which is larger than the rest.

You can buy sweet chestnuts which tend to be uniform in size. Wild chestnuts are often smaller, and you may need to persevere to find a tree with plump, juicy chestnuts. Keep your eyes peeled, as the effort is definitely worth it.

Names around the world

French Châtaignier
German Süße Kastanienbaum
Spanish Castaña dulce
Welsh Castanwydd melys
Polish Kasztan jadalny
Swedish Äkta kastanj
Your name for this plant:

....

Roasted Sweet Chestnuts

Any person with good taste (like me) will tell you that chestnuts are one of the tastiest treats on the planet, no matter what you do with them. They can be ground into a fine flour or candied, or – best of all – roasted over a real fire, either indoors or out.

Makes as many as you can find!
as many chestnuts as you can forage, washed (discard any with holes)
butter, for dipping
salt, to taste

❶ Preheat the oven to 220°C/425°F/Gas Mark 7 (or heat a barbecue or wood fire outdoors until it has died down and the embers are glowing).
❷ While you are waiting for the oven to heat or the fire to reach the correct stage, split the chestnut skins with a sharp knife. Place in a roasting pan and roast in the hot oven (or place in a heavy cast-iron pan over the glowing embers of your barbecue or fire) for 20–30 minutes, until tender.

❸ Try one of the nuts first to see if they are done. To do this, take one out using a long-handled spoon or oven glove, and let it cool for a minute or so until you can handle it without burning yourself. Crack the nut open – the contents should be soft enough to bite into.
❹ Let the nuts cool a little, then crack off the skins. Dip the inner kernels in a little butter and salt and eat just as they are.

Linden Tree
Tilia x europaea

Habitat: Parkland, the grounds of country houses and stately homes, along some city roadsides

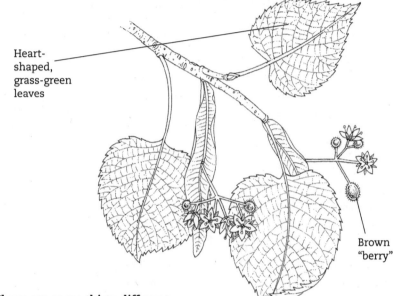

Heart-shaped, grass-green leaves

Brown "berry"

There are some thirty different species of Tilia, which is also called the Lime Tree, although this name has nothing to do with the green citrus fruit of the same name! The "Linden" or "Lime" part of this tree's name comes from the word "linde", which means the same thing in many languages: "flexible". This is because the timber of the tree is soft and easy to carve. "Tilia" means "broad", and refers to the shape of the leaf.

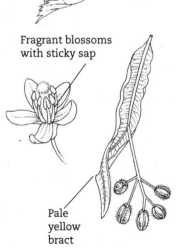

Fragrant blossoms with sticky sap

Pale yellow bract

How can I recognize a Linden Tree and where can I find one?

The Linden is a tall tree, with an average height of 30m (100ft). It has smooth, heart-shaped leaves with lightly serrated edges, up to 8cm (3in) in width, and coming to a point at the end. In spring, the tree is covered in yellow blossoms, which have a strongly fragrant scent a bit like honey. Each little bundle of flowers has a long, pale bract (a sort of leaf) underneath it. Later in the year, the tree bears round fruits, which are carried in pairs on a long stem growing from the centre of the bract.

These lovely trees can be found in the grounds of large houses and stately homes, as well as in parks and along roadsides in some cities. If, on a hot summer's day, you're out for a walk and you realize there is an exquisite scent wafting towards you, have a look round to see if you can see a tall tree frothing with yellow blossoms. The scent could well be that of the Linden-Tree blossoms. The blossoms are likely to be covered in bees, which simply love the taste of the nectar. Try eating a flower yourself – they

are delicious. Cars parked under this tree suffer from the sticky sap produced by the insects that feed on the nectar; this goo smells lovely but is difficult to remove!

Serving suggestions

You can eat the very young raw leaves of Linden. They have a cool flavour, rather like cucumber. In many parts of the world, the blossoms are used to make a tea, which can be quite expensive to buy in stores. Look out for the picture of the blossom and the bract on the box. Save your money, though, because it's very easy to make your own Linden-Blossom Tea (see p.201).

Names around the world

French	Tilleul
German	Linden
Spanish	Arbol de tilo
Welsh	Palalwyfen
Polish	Lipa, Tilia
Swedish	Lind

Your name for this plant:

....

Linden-Blossom Tea

The easiest of recipes. Simply pick some open blossoms on a warm sunny day – you can use them as they are or dry them out to use later.

Makes as many cups as you can find blossoms!

as many fresh linden blossoms as you can forage

milk and sugar (optional)

❶ For fresh tea: add ½ teaspoon of flowers per person to a teapot of freshly boiled water. Steep for 5 minutes. It will taste lovely.

❷ For dried tea: spread the blossoms out on a clean cloth (a dish towel is fine) to dry. They will take a week or more to dry out properly, since they're so sticky. Be patient – when you can crumble them without getting sticky fingers, they're done. Make sure they really are dry before storing them in an airtight jar.

❸ To make the tea, add 1 teaspoon of dried blossoms per person to a teapot and add boiling water. Steep for 5 minutes, then pour through a tea strainer into cups. Try it without milk or sugar first, but add some to taste if you prefer.

COASTAL
PLANTS

About Coastal Plants

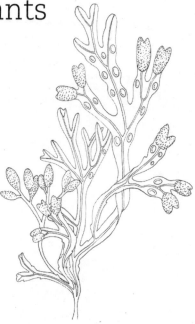

For many people, seaweeds are not much more than an interesting curiosity – just one of many aspects of a trip to the coast, like seashells, interesting pebbles, the flotsam of the ocean, candyfloss and fun rides. But in many parts of the world, these strange-looking plants are considered to be very useful as food, so much so that they're used on a daily basis (Japan is a very good example of a nation that loves to use seaweeds in cooking). The seaweeds included in this section have been chosen because they are all common and relatively easy to find.

The good news is that there are no poisonous seaweeds in shallow shoreline areas. However, common sense will tell you not to collect these plants from obviously polluted beaches or places where there are sewage outlet pipes. It is also important to remember that freshwater inland waterways (such as rivers, streams and canals) do sometimes have poisonous plants growing alongside them.

All seaweeds contain traces of minerals and vitamins which are useful for us. These include iodine (which helps control our metabolism as well as helping make our bones strong), iron (which helps carry oxygen from our lungs to the rest of our bodies) and potassium (which helps regulate the amount of water in our bodies). This explanation is very brief, by the way, otherwise this book wouldn't have any space to talk about plants and foraging! If you're planning a trip to the seaside to gather seaweeds, remember to check the local tides to make sure the sea is "out". Gathering other coastal plants is not quite so tide-related, but it is still worth checking, especially if you're making a special trip.

And if you do forget to check, and find that the tide is in and all the seaweeds are inaccessible, then at the very least you can treat yourself to an ice cream.

There's one other very useful thing you can do at the beach: that is to have a competition to see who can collect the most waste plastic washed up on the shore, with the objective of taking it to be properly disposed of at a recycling centre.

You might think that this sounds like a different sort of foraging, and you'd be right! But it's a very important one. Plastic doesn't break down like wood or paper, but breaks up into tiny little pieces that are very hard and sharp. These pieces can do a lot of harm to animals and, in particular, birds.

Even if the rubbish wasn't produced specifically by you or your family, it was certainly created by human beings. We are responsible for it, and only we can solve the problem. And a good thing that can happen is that, when other people see what you're doing, they're often reminded to start doing it too.

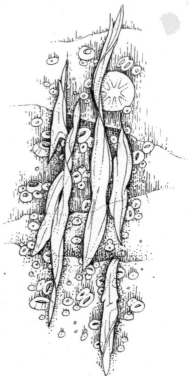

Bladderwrack
Fucus vesiculosus

Habitat: Sea and seashore

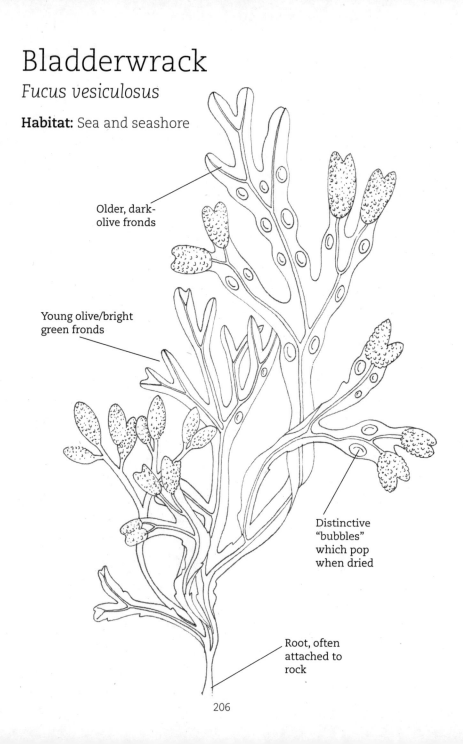

Older, dark-olive fronds

Young olive/bright green fronds

Distinctive "bubbles" which pop when dried

Root, often attached to rock

The name of this plant contains both Latin and Greek words. Fucus comes from the Greek word "phykos", which means "seaweed". Vesiculosus is Latin and means "with bladder".

There are several seaweeds with the word "wrack" in their names. It's possible that this comes from an old word: "wrecan", meaning "driven by the tide". This is the origin of the word "wreck" too, meaning "something that is damaged" or "to damage".

> ## Names around the world
>
> **French** Varech vesiculeux, Fucus vesiculeux
>
> **German** Blasentang
>
> **Spanish** Sargazo
>
> **Welsh** Gwymon codog
>
> **Polish** Morszczyn pęcherzykowaty
>
> **Swedish** Blåstång
>
> **Your name for this plant:**
>
> ....

How can I recognize Bladderwrack and where can I find it?

Searching for Bladderwrack seaweed is a good excuse for a lovely afternoon examining the seashore, wherever you happen to be.

Fresh Bladderwrack is bright green in colour, but also has shades of olive, as well as earthier brown tones.

It is found on the shoreline, clinging to rocks, left behind by the retreating tide. You'll see that the plant has a tough, flat "root" attached to the rock; it's tempting to try to detach the plant from the root, but this will damage it. Simply cut off the "leaves", a little from each plant, and don't use the tough root.

Detangle a Bladderwrack and you'll find elegant fronds, rather beautiful, with those distinctive "bubbles" that give the plant the "bladder" part of its name. These air-filled pouches come in pairs – some large, some small – and help the plant's fronds to float in the sea. When dried out, the air pouches of the Bladderwrack can be "popped" – a satisfying pastime.

Serving suggestions

The flavour of Bladderwrack, whichever way you use it, is distinctly salty and fishy-tasting. Used sparingly in a stock (the base of a soup or stew), it will add a vibrant, distinctive flavour. You might want to try making a chowder, which is a fish-based soup.

The intensely salty flavour of seaweed means that a little goes a long way – use just a small amount to start with, until you see how you like it.

You can dry Bladderwrack in a low oven (which will turn it a black colour) and grind it into a fine powder that can be used in the same way as salt and pepper – that is, as a seasoning – and which is really tasty. Remember that a little bit goes a long way since it is very salty!

Sprinkle your Bladderwrack powder sparingly on various dishes: salads, pasta, risotto or baked potatoes.

You can also cut off bite-sized pieces of fresh Bladderwrack and toast them to make "chips", which are lovely dipped in hummus or salsa. Simply place on a baking sheet and toast in a hot oven for 10–15 minutes, or until crisp.

(By the way, don't try to toast it in a toaster – the little pieces will fall through the grille and stick to the bottom, glue-ing themselves to the metal a little more every time you try to make "normal" toast, impossible to remove and making the kitchen smell very weird!)

Dulse
Palmaria palmata

Habitat: Sea and seashore

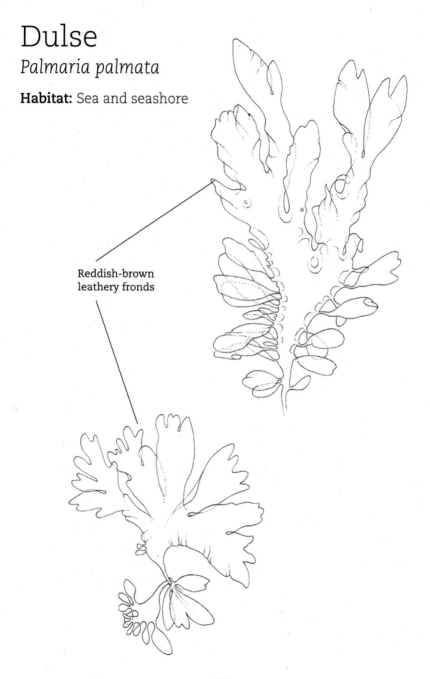

Reddish-brown
leathery fronds

How can I recognize Dulse and where can I find it?

Another seaweed, Dulse has wavy fronds (just like Bladderwrack) and can also be found "rooted" onto rocks or attached to the sea bed. However, Dulse is a distinctly reddish-brown colour – a good way to identify it from a distance. The leathery fronds can grow up to 50cm (20in) long. At low tide, you'll see Dulse stranded on the beach midway between the high and low tide lines. You may also see Dulse just beneath the water, where the fronds waft about very elegantly. You can find this seaweed all year round but it is at its best during the early months of spring. Fresh young Dulse can be compared to a young red lettuce, the kind with curly leaves. In fact, the name "Dulse" comes from a Celtic root word, "dillisk", meaning "leaf of the water".

Serving suggestions

Just like all seaweeds, Dulse is rich in vitamins and minerals that help keep you healthy.

In some parts of the world, people still dry out Dulse by draping it along a wall. If you prefer, you can dry freshly-harvested Dulse by separating out the strands and pegging them up on an outdoor washing line on a hot, sunny day. Break up the dried-out pieces into the size of crisps and see whether you like them. Some people say it tastes a bit like bacon.

In theory, Dulse can also be eaten raw. But, if you were to wash some fresh Dulse and try to eat it this way, I suspect you would spit it out immediately. Instead, try steaming it very gently for up to 30 minutes, testing it from time to time for taste and texture. Serve as a side dish, with a little salt and vinegar to taste. Be warned: a little goes a long way!

Names around the world

French Dulse
German Lappentang
Spanish lga dulse
Welsh Delysg
Polish Rodymeria palczasta
Swedish Dulse

Your name for this plant:

....

Laver

Porphyra linearis

Habitat: Sea and seashore

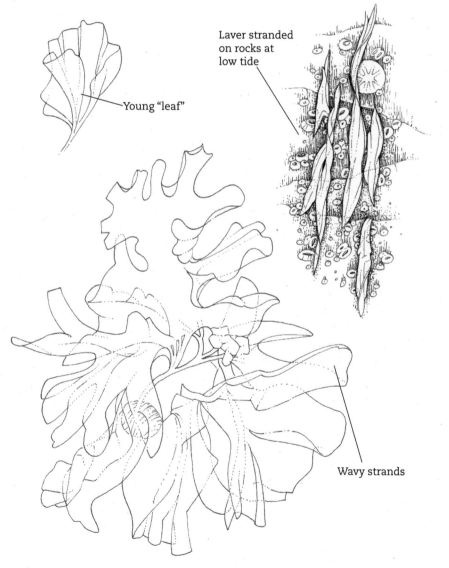

Young "leaf"

Laver stranded
on rocks at
low tide

Wavy strands

How can I recognize Laver and where can I find it?

There are several species of Laver known by the botanical name "Porphyra", which are all similar. I've chosen this one since it is common and easy to recognize.

Brown or brownish-red in colour, and comprised of thin strands only a few millimetres wide, the seaweed known as Laver is easy to recognize (and find) draped over rocks, looking like the long, shiny, gooey hair of an ageing mermaid. Try to pull apart these fronds, though, and you will discover that they are incredibly tough. This kind of Laver is more likely to be found at the top part of the beach, rather than in places which frequently get completely covered by the high tide. As the day gets hotter, the Laver dries out on the rocks and, by mid-afternoon, the plant may appear to be so dried out as to be dead; however, the incoming tide revives it and you'll see it swirling round elegantly in the water.

In Wales, laverbread (Laver boiled to a pulpy consistency – see p.213) is a traditional breakfast delicacy, available to buy canned, both in supermarkets and in gift shops. This might sound a bit horrendous – true, it is an unusual taste and one that you may not like initially, but it's worth persevering with it. It is often served mixed with oatmeal, rolled into little patties, then fried in butter with bacon.

If you have ever made sushi you may have used square, stiff sheets of nori, which is used to wrap around the rice, fish and vegetables; this is made from a different sort of Laver called Porphyra purpurea, which is also relatively easy to find, although it prefers deeper water. It has wide, thin, slippery "leaves", rather than the skinny strands of the other variety.

Names around the world

French	Nori
German	Nori
Spanish	Nori
Welsh	LLawr
Polish	Błonica sałatowa, sałata morska (sea lettuce)
Swedish	Nori

Your name for this plant:

....

If you've found yourself some Laver, you might like to try a traditional taste of Wales with this easy recipe.

Laverbread

Serves 4–6

500g (18oz) fresh laver seaweed

2 tbsp olive oil

juice of ½ lemon, or more to taste

freshly ground black pepper, to taste

thick toast, buttered, to serve

❶ Rinse and drain the seaweed several times in cold water to remove all traces of sand, grit and other debris.

❷ Place in a heavy saucepan and cook, covered with the lid, over a low heat for at least 6 hours, until the tough strands are broken down and the seaweed has become a soft, pulpy mass. You can also use a slow cooker if you have one.

❸ Add 2 tablespoons of good olive oil, the juice of half a lemon (or more to taste) and a grinding of pepper, and serve spread sparingly onto pieces of thick, buttered toast.

❹ It will keep for up to a week in a sterilized jar (see p.222) in the refrigerator.

Rock Samphire
Crithmum maritimum

Habitat: Coastal dry, rocky places, particularly cliff faces

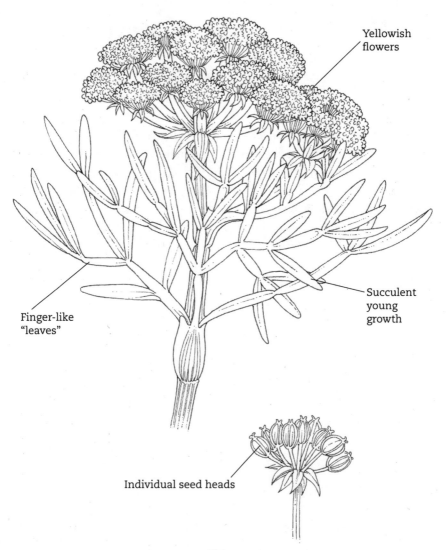

Yellowish flowers

Succulent young growth

Finger-like "leaves"

Individual seed heads

A coastal plant, the name "samphire" is derived from the French name for Saint Peter (St Pierre), who is the patron saint of the sea. Its other common names include Sea Pickle, Sea Asparagus and Sea Bean.

Incidentally, there is another edible coastal plant with a similar name, Marsh Samphire, which is not related to Rock Samphire. I prefer the taste of Rock Samphire, though, which is why I have included it here.

It's important to note that, although Rock Samphire is on the increase in coastal areas, it is a protected species, so only take a little when foraging.

Names around the world

French	Herbe Saint Pierre
German	Meerfenchel
Spanish	Cenoyo de mar, Hinojo marino, Perejil marino
Welsh	Ffenigl y môr (sea fennel) or corn carw môr (deer's horn of the sea)
Polish	Koper morski
Swedish	Strandsilja

Your name for this plant:

....

How can I recognize Rock Samphire and where can I find it?

Rock Samphire has greenish-grey, jointed leaves, which look a bit like tiny reindeer horns (hence the name in Welsh), and yellow-white flowers, which appear from late spring to early autumn (fall). Harvesting it can be tricky, since it is usually found on cliff faces, ledges and in nooks. Under no circumstances should you risk injury by clambering up cliffs faces; it grows lower down too, so keep your eyes peeled. It is said that it never grows in places where it might get its feet wet!

Serving suggestions

Samphire has a mild, salty taste and a texture somewhere between crunchy and juicy. You'll taste strong undercurrents of parsley and aniseed. The flowers are my favourite part (wash them first to remove any grit).

Rock Samphire can be used as a steamed green, rather like asparagus, and goes well with fish. Another use for it is as a pickle (see p.216).

Rock Samphire Pickle

This pickle goes very well with meats or cheeses. We also like to stir it into mashed potato!

Makes 1 x 500-g (18-oz) jar

25g (¾oz) sea salt

200g (7oz) rock samphire, thoroughly washed

500ml (17fl oz/2 cups) white wine vinegar

2 tsp whole cloves

1 cinnamon stick

1½ tsp white peppercorns

1½ tsp allspice

1 fine slice fresh ginger

❶ Add the salt to 300ml (10½fl oz/1¼ cups) water to make a brine. Add the samphire sprigs and leave to soak in the brine for 24 hours.

❷ Meanwhile, make the pickling vinegar. Put the vinegar and spices into a non-reactive saucepan with a lid. Slowly bring to a boil slowly, let boil for 2–3 minutes, then take the pan off the heat. Let stand, covered with the lid, for 2 hours (or until completely cold), then strain to remove the spices.

❸ Drain the samphire and rinse well. Transfer to a large saucepan, add the pickling vinegar and boil for 7–10 minutes, until "al dente" (soft, but with a little bite).

❹ Pour into sterilized jars (see p.222), seal tightly and keep in a cool place for 3–4 weeks before using. Once opened, eat within 1–2 weeks.

Sea Beet or Sea Spinach
Beta vulgaris maritima

Habitat: Coastal rocky places and shingle

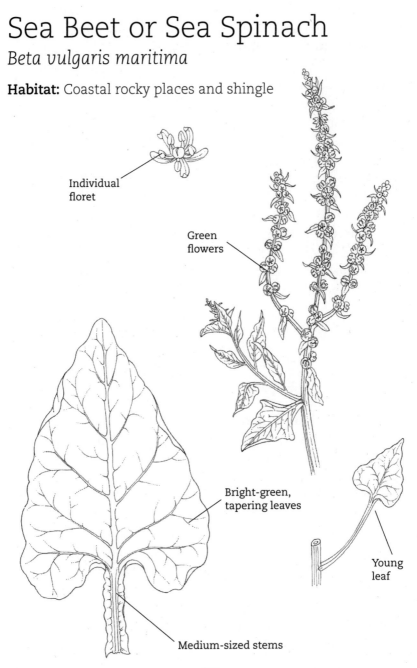

Individual
floret

Green
flowers

Bright-green,
tapering leaves

Young
leaf

Medium-sized stems

How can I recognize Sea Beet and where can I find it?

Sea Beet is a coastal plant, rather than a seaweed, and is sometimes called Sea Spinach. It does indeed look rather like "perpetual spinach", often grown by people with allotments or gardens, which has a juicier, stronger leaf than the variety of "normal" spinach that is easily found in shops. Sea Beet has bright green, tapering leaves growing from a medium-sized stem, and later in the season develops green flower shoots (or "florets") at the ends of the leafy part.

You will find Sea Beet at the part of the shore furthest away from the sea, in the rocky places where the cliffs meet the beach. Sometimes you'll see the large, thick, purple-tinted roots of the Sea Beet popping a little way out of the shingle. These roots are also edible, although tough, and to uproot any wild plant you do, of course, need to ask permission of the landowner (it's OK to harvest just the leaves).

As a wild plant, Sea Beet is plentiful, delicious and nutritious, and has been used as a valuable food source for at least 7,000 years. It is at its best in the early months of spring, however, it is very tasty all year round.

Names around the world

French Bette Maritime

German Meer Ruben

Spanish Remolacha

Welsh Betys mor

Polish Burak dziki

Swedish Strandbeta

Your name for this plant:

....

Serving suggestion

You can use Sea Beet in exactly the same way that you would spinach. Wash the leaves, pat them dry and place in a pan with a splash of water. Cook over a medium heat, with the lid on the pan, for about 8 minutes, and then have a look and a prod. You will notice that, whereas spinach would have gone soft and mushy, Sea Beet will hold its shape and texture (and will look nicer on the plate). Try the following very easy recipe (page 219) – it might well become one of your favourites!

This could easily be a meal on its own, but would also make a good side dish to a roast or baked fish.

Sea Beet and Potato Gratin

Serves 4, as a side dish

butter, for greasing
200g (7oz) fresh sea beet/sea spinach, washed and patted dry
250ml (9fl oz/1 cup) single (light) cream
1 sprig of rosemary
4 whole garlic cloves, peeled
800g (1¼lb) waxy potatoes or sweet potatoes, peeled and sliced about 4mm (⅛in) thick
50g (2oz/½ cup) grated strong cheese, such as Cheddar or Gruyère
salt and freshly ground black pepper

❶ Preheat the oven to 200°C/400°F/Gas Mark 6. Grease a 20 x 20cm (8 x 8in) ovenproof baking dish.

❷ Place the sea beet in a pan with a splash of water and cook, covered, over a medium heat for 8 minutes. Set aside to cool.

❸ Place the cream, rosemary and garlic in a small saucepan over a low heat and heat to just below boiling point. Remove from the heat, season with salt and pepper to taste and set aside to let the flavours infuse.

❹ Cover the bottom of the greased dish with half the potatoes, spread over the cooled steamed sea beet, then layer the rest of the potatoes neatly over the top (really, you've made a sandwich of the potatoes and sea beet). Pour the cream over the potatoes through a sieve (strainer) to strain out the rosemary and garlic. Top with the grated cheese and bake in the hot oven for about 50 minutes, until golden.

Further Resources

Books
There are lots of brilliant foraging books out there. Here are some of my favourites:

- Bird, F, *The Forager's Kitchen*, CICO Books, 2016
- Irving, M, *The Forager Handbook*, Ebury Press, 2009
- Mabey, R, *Food for Free*, Collins Gem, new edition 2012
- Nozedar, A, *The Hedgerow Handbook*, Square Peg, 2012
- Phillips, R, *Wild Food*, Macmillan, new edition 2014
- Rensten, J, *The Edible City*, Boxtree, 2016

If you're interested in foraging, you may also be interested in these great books about bushcraft and forest schools:
- Danks, F, and Schofield, J, *The Stick Book*, Frances Lincoln, 2012
- Worrol, J, and Houghton, P, *Play the Forest School Way*, Watkins, 2016
- Worrol, J, and Houghton, P, *A Year of Forest School*, Watkins, 2018
- Isaac, D, *101 Things for Kids to do Outside*, Kyle Books, 2014

Bags & containers for foraging
There are lots of different kinds of bags or baskets that you can buy to store your foraged finds. It's easy to find cotton or hessian bags – lots of supermarkets sell them cheaply at the checkout. Using plastic bags isn't great for foraging as the plastic can cause plants to "sweat". However, if you're gathering berries, a plastic tub with a lid is very useful. Baskets can be bought at charity shops and craft fairs. My basket was made for me by a wonderful lady in Wales, called Heather Dickens (no website, but search online under Heather Dickens Willow Baskets).

Website
Please also see my website, for tips and information about all aspects of foraging, along with a directory of images of all the plants in this book at various times in the season:
www.breaconbeaconsforaging.com
Look under the heading 'Foraging with Kids'. Please feel free to contact me there too!

Disclaimer

Although foraging is a wonderful pastime for all ages, it is important to remember that it is not without its hazards, as some plants (and fungi in particular) are poisonous. Care has been taken to ensure that none of the plants included in this book are poisonous, or resemble any plant which is harmful – with two exceptions. Those are:

• **HORSE CHESTNUT TREE** No part of the tree is edible. It has been included because its fruits (conkers) make a really good soap. The entry clearly states that conkers shouldn't be eaten.

• **RAMSONS** bear a resemblance to two toxic plants (Lily of the Valley and Colchicum autumnale [Autumn Crocus]). There is a failsafe way to identify the 'right' plant, which is clearly explained in the entry.

GENERAL DISCLAIMER: The material contained in this book is set out in good faith for general guidance and no liability can be accepted for loss or expense incurred in relying on the information given. In particular this book is not intended to replace expert medical advice. This book is for informational purposes only and is for your own personal use and guidance. It is not intended to diagnose, treat, or act as a substitute for professional medical advice. The author is not a medical practitioner, and professional advice should be sought if desired before embarking on any health-related programme.

Cooking Notes

Some of the recipes in this book, such as jam, require heating the food to very hot temperatures. Always check with your parents (or other tame grown-ups) before you start to make anything and ensure that you are supervised. Do invite those tame grown-ups to help you, but do also clean up after yourself!

While the majority of the equipment needed is the standard sort of stuff that most kitchens have, there are a few specialist bits of kit that might be handy, especially if you fancy making jams, chutneys or pickles.

These include:
- a large, heavy pan with a lid
- a jam (preserving) thermometer
- jam (preserving) jars and waxed paper discs (if you are planning to sell your jam, you MUST use brand-new sterilized jars – see below)
- a jelly-straining kit, including a jelly bag
- a good wire-mesh sieve (strainer)

Sterilizing

If using second-hand jam jars, make sure there's no gunk left on the insides of the lids, then wash both jars and lids in a dishwasher (if you have one, and if you have permission to use it). Alternatively, wash well in hot, soapy water. Rinse thoroughly, then place upside-down on a baking pan lined with baking parchment. Dry in an oven set at 175°C/350°F/Gas Mark 4 for 10 minutes. Handle with care when removing them from the oven.

Never put cold ingredients into hot jars, or hot ingredients into cold jars, as glass jars might shatter.

Acknowledgements

Thanks to all the Wizards and Stars

My favourite place in the world is up in the mountains of the Brecon Beacons, in Wales. It is the wild beauty of the land and skies in this part of the planet that really inspires my foraging (and other) adventures. In particular, there are two little streams, the Taf Fechan (or "little Taf") and the Taf Fawr ("big Taf"), that intrigue me. These streams trickle through the heather-clad uplands, gathering momentum until they come together to make one river, called the Taf, that becomes more and more impressive as it flows on downhill through remote wooded valleys, past houses and on through villages, towns, and finally through the great city of Cardiff, where the river meets the sea.

In the same way that the River Taf has two sources, so does this book. The first source is the landscape; and whether that landscape is remote open country where few people live, or a crowded urban place with a massive population, really doesn't matter. The other source is the thousands of people, of all ages and backgrounds, who have, over the last few years, joined me on a foraging walk to find out about the plants that form a vital part of our lives. If you are one of these people – thank you. You have taught me many, many things, not just about plants, but also about history; your families; dotty superstitions, funny stories, or names for plants that you hadn't thought about for years; recipes for foods and medicines; all sorts of wonderful information that always makes these walks such a huge pleasure, no matter where I go.

I'd like to thank the team at Watkins, especially Chris Wold for contacting me to see if I had any ideas; Jo Lal for her enthusiasm about this one in particular; Dan Hurst for his brilliant ideas, upbeat encouragement and enthusiasm; and Georgie Hewitt and Karen Smith for designing this lovely book. Thanks, too, to Vicky Hartley, Vikki Scott and Lucia Garavaglia. Hats off to Emily Preece-Morrison for your eagle-eyed editing expertise and endless patience. I'd also like to thank Marli, Asa,

Ethan, Anouk, Oscar, Freddie, Ursula and Rhys for sharing their boundless energy and enthusiasm on our foraging walk. My gratitude, also, to Laura West and Veronique Baxter at David Higham Associates.

The exquisite illustrations in this book were created by Lizzie Harper (www.lizzieharper.co.uk). I'm so glad that she was able to do them, as they're not only impeccably accurate drawings, but very beautiful too.

I am very lucky to have friends who were willing to help with the plant names in languages other than English. I wanted to include these to show that the plants in this book belong to all the world and that, largely, their names have shared meanings. I wish I could have added more! I'm very grateful to author Myfanwy Alexander (Welsh); M. Deby Crowhurst and the Livarot French Conversation Group (French); Florentina James (Spanish); Katja Katholing-Bloss (www.katjakatholing-bloss.com) (German); Ania Ciolek (Polish); and Henrik Elmer (Swedish).

Rachael Phillips (www.rachaelphillips.me) has been an invaluable friend and designed my website. She deserves a massive bouquet of flowers for putting up with my constant barmy questions.

Several people kindly allowed me to share recipes. Thank you to Christina Marocco for the Dandelion Frittata, and to Suzanne Davies for the Poached Plums and the Spicy Plum Sauce.

Thanks to my friends and colleagues at The Association of Foragers (www.foragers-association.org.uk), especially the legendary Henry Ashby, whose life story would make the most spectacular movie!

As I'm writing this, just a moment ago, Liam Fitzpatrick popped his head around the door to ask me what I wanted for dinner. I reminded him that it was my turn to cook. "You write the book. I'll cook," he said. This is lucky, since he makes the most delicious food I've ever eaten. Thank you Liam!